floral Design Concepts

with African Violets

& Other Gesneriads

Ruth Jo McCoy

*These basic principles and procedures may be used with other delicate plant
material and fresh- cut blossoms including Fuschias, Miniature Roses,
Specie Orchids and other petite growing plants.*

Printed in the United States of America

Typography by Nick Smith
Proofreading by Suzanne Gibson

at the offices of *the California Tech*, Pasadena, California.

Printed by
ANDREWS PRINTING COMPANY, INC.
2141 Bixby Road,
Lakewood, California 90712
(213) 636-9149

Library of Congress Catalog Card Number: 85-50215

ISBN:0-9614604-0-7

Floral Design Concepts With African Violets and Other Gesneriads

By Ruth Jo McCoy

Illustrated by Bjo Trimble
Photographs by Rita Oyan Ractliffe

Published by

TRI-COLOR PRESS
3963 Wilshire Boulevard,
Suite 600
Los Angeles, California 90010

Cover photograph by Rita Dyan Ractliffe

COVER DESIGN: *A Florida cypress "knee" shelters a porcelain Madonna, with two-toned "Valencia" African violet as focal point. Pussywillow and treated spiral eucalyptus branches form background line material, with sprays of dried wild grass for accent. This design is a many-time blue and tri-color ribbon winner.*

DEDICATION

To our long-suffering and patient husbands, John McCoy and John Trimble, for the cups of coffee, comfort, kitchen duty, encouragement and love, without whom this book would have certainly happened but with lots less enjoyment in its production.

—Ruth Jo McCoy, author
—Bjo Trimble, illustrator

AESCHYNANTHUS HILDEBRANDII

forward

My intent in this book is to make Design with African violets and other gesneriads grown primarily by horticultural hobbyists as much fun and as full of excitement as your imagination will allow.

Ruth Jo McCoy

INTRODUCTION

The African violet is well-established as America's favorite houseplant. Its fascinating introduction into America from its origin in East Africa is valuable history. Those of us who have watched its phenomenal growth over the past 40 years marvel at its unique place in the horticultural world today. Not only have we pursued perfection in growing, grooming and showing these versatile plants but our AVSA members have shown great ingenuity in using the delicate African violet blossoms and plants in competitive arrangements and artistic plantings.

Classes were established in many early shows but often, clumsily arranged designs by the beginner appeared. Although our Judges Handbook established rules, no clear and specific instructions were available. Most winning designs and arrangements were entered by talented individuals who possessed prior knowledge of flower arrangement, thus providing over the years the many beautiful arrangements we have been privileged to enjoy.

Jo McCoy is the first individual to my knowledge to come forth with a very instructive, valuable book on design. *Floral Design Concepts with African Violets and Other Gesneriads*, this book, will be a most welcome reference book to all who undertake creative arrangement to enhance our popular African violet and the entire gesneriad family.

Jo is an individual of many talents; she is a well-known, very active Life Member of the African Violet Society of America, Inc., and a Life Time Judge and teacher and also senior American Gloxinia and Gesneriad Society judge. She was honored at our 33rd African Violet Society of America, Inc. convention in Colorado with the coveted Ruth Carey Award for her active work in organizing many African violet clubs—all are affiliate chapters of our society.

We met Jo on a trip to Hawaii in 1962, became fast friends, and have remained friends ever since. She is a high-spirited, inspiring individual with so much talent and sensitivity toward helping people to enjoy their plants.

One of her greatest assets is her daughter Bjo Trimble, who is a professional writer and illustrator. It must make her proud and give great satisfaction for Bjo to do the many illustrations for this book.

Design Concepts is a long-awaited book that will take the newest beginners interested in floral arrangement of any kind and especially our favorite plant, the African violet and its relatives. Designing is an art form that brings personal satisfaction and joy of beauty and accomplishment.

We salute you, Jo, for being talented and brave enough to share your knowledge and experience with each of us who pursue beauty of plant life in any form.

—Anne and Frank Tinari

Past & present Presidents, African Violet Society of America
Owners, Tinari Greenhouses

COLUMNEA "YELLOW BIRD"

IN APPRECIATION

Thanks to

Doris Ashley
Frances Batcheller, AGGS Chairman of Shows and Judging
Ken and Frances Fleshman
Ed & Marti Ish
Linda Jorgensen
Dorothy Kahrmann
Loree Lange
Alan La Vergne
Madge Lilliquist
John McCoy, my loving Husband (but a lousy fisherman)
Rita Ractliffe
Jesse Smith
Frank and Anne Tinari
Bju Trimble, my patient Daughter, and her husband John
Margaret Waguespack

AFRICAN VIOLETS ARE GESNERIADS

To avoid repeating both names throughout this book, I will refer to both African violets and gesneriads in general as "gesneriads".

Floral Design Concepts with African violets and Other Gesneriads

CHAPTER I

CHAPTER II

CHAPTER III

CHAPTER IV

Jo McCoy with a few of her prize ribbons

"Guess I should give her flowers more often!"

CHAPTER I

Gift-Wrapping Your Gesneriads

Why should one design with delicate flowers and plants? Because the more unusual plants and flowers are most in demand but generally not available in florist or gift shops. African violets and Gesneriads are decidedly different, easy to grow and stay in bloom most all year with the proper care and feeding program. Many gesneriads are grown from tubers or rhizomes, so if they get too dry they just go dormant for a short period of time (they should be kept slightly moist at this time to

1

prevent dehydration, then start adding water and food). They will come up and bloom again in a short time. Some fibrous-rooted types are African Violets, *Aeschynanthus*, *Episcia*, *Streptocarpus*, and there are many others just as fascinating and colorful. The virtue of this genus is the colorful and unusual types of foliage and blossoms. They blend with any type of home decoration, and create a novel conversation piece, sure to please the recipient.

What to do with the flowers after you've created a design: give them as decorated or boxed gifts. Put bows and extra flowers in living plants, offer a few flowers in a bud vase, or make fabulous gifts for:

Ceramic teddybear container with living Sinningia plant for baby.

Babies and Births: There are all kinds of amusing infant ceramic containers on the market, in which you can arrange fresh flowers or plants. Select something suitable to the occasion, and (since mommy will have to take care of the plant, anyway) attach a small toy for baby. The container might be selected with an eye to its usefulness after the flowers are gone: a safety-pin jar or cannister would be one idea. Almost always, the infant gift container becomes a keepsake to be handed to the child for his progeny.

A sentimental gift for the new mother is the "pillow corsage" which can be placed within easy view. A few scented blossoms might be added for extra effect. This particular gift idea is so unique

that everyone in the hospital will be interested in seeing it.

Bottle garden gift for a man, with tiny bottle of whiskey tied to bow.

Men: Most people don't think about giving flowers or plants to men, but there are many, many males who enjoy raising African violets and all the rest of the gesneriad family. You could design a boutonniere for your favorite man to wear to work, just to brighten his day. A single flower on his desk can remind him of you, all day long. It's a cheerful way to say "Have a happy day."

A more lasting gift would be an unusual planting, such as a dish garden, terrarium or bottle garden. Since these plantings need very little care, they are perfect for the busy male.

When designing an arrangement or planting for a man, use strong lines and materials with bold colors. These are considered "masculine" in feeling, and are the most likely to appeal to the average male.

Sinningia Canescens, undecorated.

2

Some of the occasions to present a floral design or planting to your favorite man would be: birthdays, anniversaries, holidays, promotions, service recognition, getting a new office, a grand opening, hospitalization, or just to say "I want you to know I love you."

Women: Body flowers can be worn anywhere a woman wants to place them. Corsages, hairpieces, wristlets, nosegays and mini-nosegays (which can be carried or even worn on the finger!) are popular means of wearing flowers.

Gifts for women can include any kind of planting, as well as floral arrangements of cut flowers. Every woman loves to be told she's loved, and there are few better ways to show it than with flowers and living plants. One of the most romantic proposals I've ever heard of was the presentation of the ring in the bottom of a miniature pool of water in a tiny terrarium. Both the people involved were avid plant-lovers.

For a "feminine" floral arrangement, use a horizontal or curved vertical line in your design.

Teens: Young people like the unusual flowers, such as mini-nosegays, and other body flowers that can be worn in a unique manner. Most teen girls are thrilled to get flowers, and feel very "grown-up" when they are the recipient of a corsage or floral arrangement. Design something in romantic pastels or bright, vivacious colors for teens. Unless they have an enthusiasm for living

Sinningia Canescens, decorated with bow, and three long-stemmed rosebuds, for gift-giving.

plants, a permanent arrangement may not be of much interest to them.

Tussy-mussy nosegay bouquet & hair decoration for prom, wedding or other occasion.

Weddings: Flowers are needed for mass arrangements in the church and reception hall, fan-shaped designs for table and baskets, altar arrangements, aisle decorations, candelabra decorations, and anywhere else flowers can be used for this happy occasion. Personal flowers would include the bride's and attendant's bouquets, groom's and groomsmen's boutonnieres, corsages and boutonnieres for all the relatives who deserve one, and corsages for friends. Flowers and fresh foliage are a traditional part of our weddings, and they can be made even more beautiful with gesneriads.

Engagements: Even the simplest celebrations call for a corsage for the bride-to-be; a more elaborate event calls for table decorations, floral arrangements in the room, individual flowers, boutonnieres and corsages.

Birthdays, Anniversaries, Holidays and Surprises: Attractive gifts can be incorporated into a planting or floral design, for the appropriate occasion. This book is concerned with developing the creativity to whip up a floral design at a moment's notice for any kind of event. Adding flowers and plants to an occasion makes it just that much more fun.

Get-Well: Bottle gardens, dish gardens, terrariums, and such plantings are the best idea for someone who is ill. Cut flowers are believed, by some medical authorities, to create bacteria in the water that might be unhealthy to patients. Fading flowers can also create depression. A cheerfully growing plant, on the other hand, is a pretty sight by a bedside. A small gift might be attached to the plant by means of a ribbon or bow.

Pets: Don't laugh! Remember, I am a professional florist who has delivered floral arrangements and plants to pets for birthdays, holidays, to the pet hospital, and the pet cemetery. Often, I would get an order from owners on their vacations to send

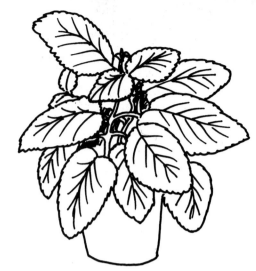

Sinningia Regina undecorated.

a floral gift with a card reading, "Love Muggsy, we miss you so much!"

This is not as funny as it may seem to a person who is not fond of animals. Many people have a very strong paternal feeling for their pets. In our own household we have two very large and very spoiled alley cats that allow us to live here.

Pet-shaped containers can be obtained that will hold a plant or an arrangement, or a pet dish will make a fine temporary planter, too. A potted African violet or *sinningia*, or any small plant, makes a fine gift (at least to the pet owner), and a pet toy or a doggie-chew can be attached to the plant with a ribbon. A spray of *aeschynanthus* in a bud vase would make a nice gift.

Sympathy: Sprays, wreaths, floral pillows, and set pieces can be made from gesneriads. Decorated plants and arrangements for the home of the bereaved can go into a memory garden, and are usually much appreciated.

If you think that gesneriads are too delicate for this type of design, may be it is because you have never seen it done. I designed and constructed a casket piece of African violet plants for a four year old girl. It was to be shipped with the remains to Texas, so I chose to use the whole plants. I had several plants of the soft blue "Lullaby" African violet in bloom. So I made a base of damp long-fiber spagnum moss, attached to a neutral-colored burlap. The plants were removed from the pot, the root ball encased in the toe part of old nylon hose, and placed in the moss. Keeping to the same

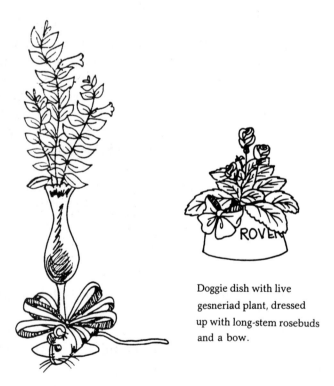

Doggie dish with live gesneriad plant, dressed up with long-stem rosebuds and a bow.

Bud vase with three gesneriads,

and a catnip mouse toy, for kitty.

Sinningia Regina decorated with bow, and one long-stemmed rosebud, for gift-giving.

delicate texture of the violets, I added the draping effect of *Alsobia dianthaflora* and sprigs of *Springiori Miorrii* fern, and finished with delicate bows and streamers of soft blue ribbon to match the "Lullaby" blossoms.

When the mother returned, she told me that she had repotted the plants and presented them to the grandmothers and aunts. The *alsobia* cuttings had been given to other members of the family, to start as new plants.

Never underestimate the dimension of love.

Institutions: Such places as rest homes, convalescent hospitals, etc., need all the cheering up they can get. Bottle gardens, bubble bowls, terrariums, hanging gardens, and dish gardens are very good gifts for someone in an institution of this kind. As with "get-well" gifts, cut flowers are not always recommended, as fading flowers sometimes create depression, especially with the elderly or critically ill. Still, for special occasions, a corsage or boutonniere is a very cheering gift, even if the recipient isn't going anywhere. It seems to make a person feel a bit perkier.

Presenting floral gifts to friends is very easy. The simplest method is to just hand them the flowers and smile. This is guaranteed to create the desired result of surprise and delight.

However, there are fancier methods of presentation: repot a pretty African violet or other gesneriad into a decorative planter, or wrap the original pot with foil or pretty paper, or place it in a box, surrounded by colored tissue.

If you wish to give a specific variety of plant and it doesn't oblige by blooming at the time, wire and tape an orchid or rosebud or three, and stick them into the pot with a pick. Or place the blooms in a waterpick, and insert it in the soil of the plant.

Or add a small bouquet of gesneriad blossoms from a more obliging plant.

Then add a bow of suitable color, with perhaps an appropriate card attached. a small gift (such as a box containing an engagement ring!) may be wired to the bow, or tucked into the foliage. Please refer to Chapter IV for instructions in making a proper ribbon bow.

Any potted plant may be given that extra "gift" look with merely a pretty bow added; by using the design suggestions in this book, you can make the plant look like the best of gifts!

There are many occasions for giving flowers and plants as gifts; happy events and sad ones. Floral arrangements and living plants can be a silent comfort, and in many cases a sentimental memory for someone.

Growing gesneriads is such a fascinating and worthwhile experience, it is natural to want to share them.

5

"Honey, I **promise** to keep the plant room under control, after this!"

6

CHAPTER II

Beginning: The Mechanics

You need a solid work space, a firm table or counter top, preferably in an area not to be disturbed, so the design may remain in place for evaluation.

TOOLS:

A good firm-bladed paring knife or pocket knife will do; a true florist's knife has a curve at the end, but is difficult to obtain.

Florist's knife

A sharp X-acto knife is also useful for some design work and cutting. Be sure to keep all knives out of the reach of children and pets.

The reason you should learn to use a knife, instead of scissors, when designing, is that scissors crush the stem so they will not draw water. This means that the flowers and foliage used in your design will fade faster, and possibly cost you points in a show. A knife will make a clean diagonal cut across the stem, allowing the flower to stay fresher longer. Though it takes a little practice to use a knife as handily as scissors, the effort will be well worth it, when you see the results.

Pliers may be any household pliers, found in your spouse's tool box. Wire cutters may be obtained in the same manner—either heavy-duty or small hobby or jeweler's cutters may be used.

Heavy-duty wire cutter   Jeweler's wire cutter

Pliers are necessary when twisting wire firmly around stems, picks and bows. After awhile, your fingers will get very sore and very tired, if you insist on twisting wire by hand. Also, using pliers will make certain anything in your design that is wired will *stay wired throughout the show, or the length of time the arrangement is supposed to be stable.*

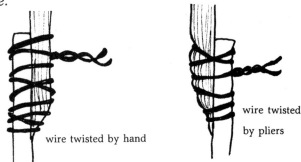

wire twisted by hand

wire twisted by pliers

Tweezers may be any pair of tweezers that happen to be handy; they will be used to hold short or soft stems in place while pushing the stem down on the sharp point of the pin frog.

Again, it may seem quicker to just push the stems onto the pin frog by hand, but the constant little pricks on the fingers will result in tired hands. This in turn will only encourage mistakes. Better to learn how to use tools correctly than to learn sloppy design habits.

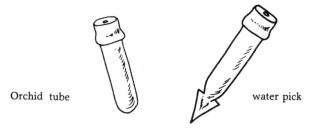

Orchid tube

water pick

Water picks are small 3" long plastic containers about ½" in diameter, with a pointed end. The open end has a rubber or plastic cap with a small hole in the top where the flower can be pushed in. The pick is filled with water, the cap snapped on, and then used to keep individual flowers fresh. The pointed end may be pushed into various parts of the design. This is the method by which fresh flowers are added to a potted plant that has no flowers on its own.

Orchid tubes are water picks that have no pointed end. They were designed primarily to keep orchids fresh, but work admirably for gesneriads. Several gesneriad stems will fit into the cap of one orchid tube or water pick.

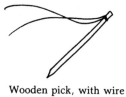

Wooden pick, with wire

Wooden pick with net pouf, as seen from back

Wooden picks are available in many lengths, from 2" to 8" long, with an 8" fine wire attached to the blunt end. The other end is pointed, so that it can be pushed into the design. These are used for extending the height of your line material. Flowers in water picks may be placed higher in a design, using wooden picks. Also used to attach bows to plants and designs.

Pin frogs come in all sizes (so do real frogs)

The pin frog does not jump. It is made of heavy metal, has a weighted base with sharp points on top. Used to secure stems of flowers and foliage by pushing the stems firmly on the sharp points. This gives stability to the design and holds all material in place.

The pin frog is secured to the design base with a strip of florists' clay around the bottom of the pin frog. This is then "screwed" gently but firmly straight down onto the base. In this manner, you can assure that when the pin frog has been loaded with foliage, it will not tip over. When the need for that design is over, the clay may be rolled off the base and the pin frog without harming either.

Placing florist's clay around bottom of pin frog

8

Placing pin frog on base.

Chicken wire should be cut 5" wide and any length feasible to crush and insert in tall container. This takes the place of a pin frog in cases where a frog would not be easy to work with.

Usually, chicken wire is used in deep containers instead of a pin frog, which would be difficult to reach. It is not possible, as my daughter can tell you, to place all the flowers and foliage on a pin frog and *then* drop the whole thing into a tall container. I suppose I should be glad she can at least draw cartoons.

Chicken wire is also handy to roll for low designs on a base. Plants and foliage can be stuck into the wire to create a very naturalistic design, which is also sturdy enough to take a bit of handling.

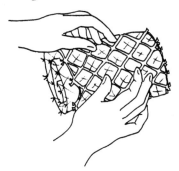

Roll of chicken wire

A soft 2" sash brush will be useful to keep the design clean, and the arrangement dusted.

Dust particles on a completed design can result in a loss of judges' points if you've entered your creation in a show. Keep your work area brushed clean, and keep your design clean as you work on it.

Small ceramic figurines, keeping in mind proportion, are very important. One can lose many points in judging by ceramics being too large. A good rule of thumb is used by the

miniature doll house makers of 1" to 1' rat.

Rocks, pebbles, and sand are used for accen

Driftwood is very often used for line material, or emphasis on a particular part of the design. Also popular for designs are root knots, dried branches, desert wood (collect *only* where it's legal!) and grapevine. *Any* interesting branch can be your line material.

Towels are needed for cleaning up your work area; cloth or paper will do.

Base, with pin frog and piece of driftwood attached, ready for a design.

Bases can be driftwood, cork slabs, weathered wood, styrofoam, shallow trays, serving platters, rock slabs, shallow wicker baskets, or wicker squares, hot pads (the underside is asbestos, and can be painted with any shoe polish in the desired color), placemats, heavy cardboard cut to desired shape, picture frames (with or without the picture), mirrors.

Some shows allow draping for a background. In this case, you should probably have something which will hold up the drapery, that will not interfere with the design. Make certain you have the dimensions allowed by the show schedule, and then work out a method of holding up the drapery, either with a small box, or perhaps a picture frame, etc.

Fabric for draping in the back of a design can

bric with a dull or soft finish. Velvet, ouble-knit, solid color woolens, etc.

Background may be wood paneling, styrofoam, weathered wood, self-sticking shelving paper (such as Contac, etc.). If the color or texture is too intense, cover it with net, or sheer fabric in a lighter tone. On wood or styrofoam, use floral spray to dull the color or texture.

You can use just about any container that fits the occasion, that also fits the design in mind. Anything with a shiny finish detracts from your design and if these are being photographed, a bright finish will distort the photo. However, you take care of that with Fuller's earth, or use baby talc. On white or light-colored ceramics, or metal, use the talc. Rub the container gently with the fingers and the earth or powder. On the darker colors, use fermate, which is a type of horticultural "soot."

SUPPLIES:

Floral foam is a sponge-foam that absorbs water and is used in designs to support the flowers and stems, retaining their freshness.

This interesting material is used in containers, instead of a pin frog, in some designs. Since it holds water, it must be placed inside something waterproof to prevent it leaking liquid.

Floral foam may be dried out and used again and again. it is obtainable in most floral supply houses, some hobby shops, and from friendly local florists, who may be talked into selling you a chunk. It will eventually disintegrate from use, but if treated carefully, will last a long time.

Florist's tape is ½-inch wide waxed crepe paper, in a roll. It comes in many colors. It will stick to itself, but not to anything else. This tape comes in a roll that is easily held in the hand.

Taping flowers, wires, foliage and any of the

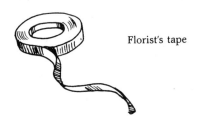

Florist's tape

"mechanics" of a design will assure a finished look. It requires only a little effort and practice to learn how to tape down a wire or stem correctly. The result in your design will be well worth it.

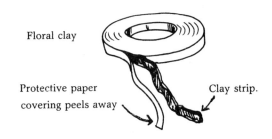

Floral clay

Protective paper covering peels away

Clay strip.

Floral clay is a very pliable substance, resembling modeling clay. Used by professionals and hobbyists in the floral field worldwide. It is packaged in a roll approximately 1" wide by ¼" thick, and is used to secure pin frogs or any type of holder in the container.

Arrangement containers may be *constructed* if you can't find one that suits the design in your mind's eye. Floral clay will peel off of almost any container, but while it is pressed onto it, will hold pieces together so they can be stacked, etc.

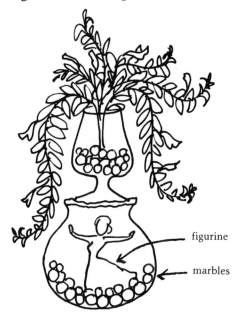

figurine

marbles

Brandy snifter & bubble bowl "glued together" with floral clay (which can be covered with ribbon or greenery)

10

Experiment first to see how steady you can make such a container, before adding the plant or cut flowers.

Also, florists' tape, which is very sticky and very sturdy, can be used to hold various pieces and containers together for an arrangement. Again, be sure the pieces are stable before adding the plants.

Candleholders can be thus combined with bowls, wine glasses and even canning jars to obtain the height desired, or to create an effect. Various components of a "construction" can be filled with marbles, a figurine, colored water, or anything else that would be safe to place on exhibit.

Florists' wire comes two ways: bare and covered. The bare wire is used anywhere it will not show in a design or arrangement. Covered wire has been wrapped in thin thread, usually in green color, but sometimes can be found in other colors. This wire is used where it might be seen in the design, and sometimes for effects requiring the wire to be in view. Depending on your design, you may use both kinds of wire at once.

Several sizes of wire are used to shape line material; the #28 wire is used to support very delicate blossoms; #20, 22 and 28 are the most commonly used by florists.

Fuller's earth is an absorbent powder, found in drug stores. Used to dull the shine on containers and bases; absorbs oil and grease. Fuller's earth is white, and used on light colors. **WARNING: Both Fuller's earth and Fermate (below) are fine dusts and prolonged inhaling of them can be dangerous.**

Fermate is also used to take the shine off containers and bases. Fermate is black, and used on dark containers. This may be obtained at garden supply shops or nurseries. Soot from the fireplace or barbeque pit will do pretty well, too, but can permanently stain the base.

Floral spray can be obtained at any floral supply house. It comes in many, many different colors. This is non-injurious to flowers and plants. It acts as a mild preservative on dried material. This is not to be used on living flowers and plants, but only on cut material.

Hand-cleaner in a pressure spray can will remove floral spray and paint, and most of the soil you would get on your hands. Your hands do get very soiled. Some of the plant material "bleeds" sticky stuff and you need to remove that from your hands before going on with the design.

Chenille craft wire is a twisted wire with 3/8" covering of fine thread to give it a fuzzy texture. Use to support line material and also a stem extender.

What NOT To Use In Designs: Do NOT use small live animals, birds, or fish. Use ceramic, clay or blown glass critters instead. Fish will not live long in an underwater design with plants which are not truly aquatic.

Do NOT use real eggs; you are inviting disaster. Use jellybeans or small round pebbles in a real nest, if you wish.

And NEVER use anything of sentimental value, or keepsakes, or valuable antiques. Not everyone visiting a show is totally honest, and a

"Well, there goes the neighborhood!"

11

pretty antique necklace or brooch may be a strong temptation.

With the best of intentions, one clever lady who found an abandoned bird nest with babies, fed and cared for them until a flower show. Then she used the nest, with the baby birds happily asleep in it, for an attractive display. Unfortunately, everyone else mistook the design; they surmised a bird's nest had been ravaged to accomplish the design. A judge burst into tears, others were very upset. The designer, puzzled by the furor, assured everyone all was well, but it was too late. Afterward, she took the baby birds home, raised them till they were ready to fly, then set them free. I am sure she never considered the harm the babies would take from thoughtless smokers, people who would touch, prod, or even pick up the birds to "see if they were real." For this reason, I recommend never using live animals, birds, fish or even insects. There are many interesting and creative ways to accomplish the desired effect in design.

A bird nest always acts as an attention point, but a few jelly beans in the appropriate color makes a fine substitute for eggs. Most eggs are soft blue, white or ecru color, so small round pebbles sometimes make better substitutes.

One lady used a valuable antique brooch in a design, and wanted the show chairman to post a guard to keep the brooch from being stolen. This is not reasonable, for while show committees take every standard precaution, it is not the responsibility of a show or the judges to police every exhibit.

It is nice to own antiques and family heirlooms, but sad as it may be, everyone is not honest. Do not risk sentimental keepsakes in a public show, but instead use them in personal designs for display to friends in your own home.

CHAPTER II

Tools and Supplies for Practice

TOOLS:
>   sharp knife
>   pliers
>   wire-cutters
>   tweezers
>   2″ sash brush
>   towels: paper or cloth
>   containers
>   pin frogs
>   chicken wire
>   fabric for draping
>   background material
>   base
>   driftwood
>   figurines
>   rocks, pebbles

SUPPLIES:
>   floral foam
>   florist's wire: #20, 22, 28
>   water picks
>   florist's tape
>   florist's clay
>   chenille craft wire
>   wooden picks
>   Fuller's earth
>   fermate
>   floral spray
>   hand-cleaner
>   talcum powder
>   shoe polish

AESCHYNANTHUS PULOVIA

CHAPTER III

Miniature, Semi-Miniature and Standard Arrangements Combining Fresh, Dried, and/or Treated Materials

*PRACTICE, PRACTICE, PRACTICE, PRACTICE,
PRACTICE, PRACTICE, PRACTICE, PRACTICE!*

If you have difficulty in thinking of creative ideas for a design, sometimes the show schedule will give you notions. Generally, shows have a theme, and they have a specific idea of what they want for that theme. Show schedules will often give not only a title but background material for that theme. Song titles are popular subjects for design themes, and are great to generate creative ideas. Religious themes, show themes, garden scenes, and nature themes (mountains, desert, woodland, etc.) are just a few of the ideas you can utilize to start a beautiful design.

Working with gesneriads, there is not a great amount of strong line material available. As gesneriads grow, they do not offer much in height,

stability and balance, so we must improvise a bit. This is the part where practice in wiring will be very beneficial. Line material can be *created* from gesneriad foliage with some judicious wiring.

However, most show schedules will state, 'with other plant material,' so line material can be supplied from such foliage as: aspidistra leaves, iris leaves, some *streptocarpus* leaves which are long and slender enough, *nematanthus, aeschynanthus*, ivy, fern, etc. Much of this material can be cut, rolled, or shaped as desired. Some of this material must be wired or trimmed to the desired shape.

Different methods of this practice are illustrated on the next page. Most show schedules will state, 'with other plant material,' so some of the other materials sometimes used are: aspidistra leaves, cut, rolled or trimmed to the desired shape; iris leaves; some *streptocarpus* leaves, which are long and slender enough. All this material takes a minimum of preparation. Submerge the whole leaf in shallow water for a few hours or overnight. This procedure causes the material to absorb the maximum of water possible, thus preserving the turgidity of the material for a prolonged period of time. When placed in the design, the stem may be placed in a shallow container of water to maintain the proper form to enhance the design.

wired foliage can be manipulated

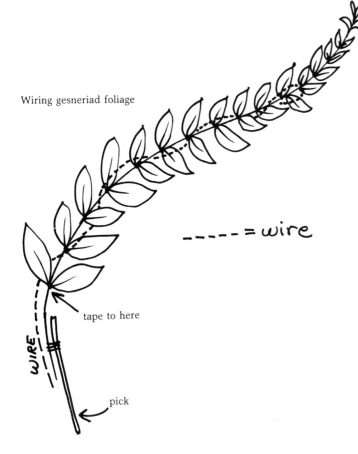

Wiring gesneriad foliage

----- = wire

tape to here

pick

Wiring a trailing stem to use as line material

Other line material that enhances a design is branches of *nematanthus, aeschynanthus*, ivy, fern, etc. These must be either wired or trimmed to the desired shape.

An example of rolled leaves can be studied in the color section.

Because gesneriads do not always produce a profusion of blooms, your practice design should

be made with ordinary garden greenery and flowers. Select a similar size to the gesneriads to be used in show design. This will save lots of time and material, and avoid wasting what is often a limited number of usable flowers.

Interior Decorating with Gesneriads

A big plus for growing gesneriads is being able to use them artistically in the home. People hesitate to cut gesneriad blossoms, or remove foliage for a cut flower arrangement, but there are many ways to use them without disturbing the growing plant or cutting the blossoms.

Consider how many times people arrange a lovely dinner party and make no plans for flowers. If a husband or arriving guest should bring flowers, this last-minute arrival makes it impossible to stop and do an arrangement. Simply putting the flowers in a vase casually is not fair to the giver or the recipient.

Candleholder with florist's clay on bottom

This idea is not time-consuming, yet can be very effective. Start with a shallow basket, about 2½" deep, and 8 × 12 inches in size. These dimensions are appropriate for a table seating 8 to 12 people. If you have single candle holders, secure them in a row with florist's clay to the

16

Digging a hole in a styrofoam block

bottom of the basket. (By the way, the basket should not have a handle if you intend to light the candles.) If you don't have candle holders, it is easy to make some with a piece of 2"-thick styrofoam, about 3" wide and 8" long. Carve three holes in the styrofoam to fit the candles. Then secure the styrofoam to the basket with florist's clay.

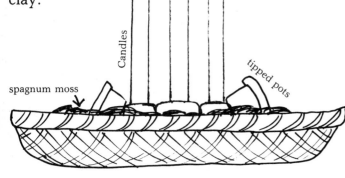

One 18" candle and two 16" ones, in the color of your choice, make a nice accent for the plants to be used. You can, of course, vary this suggestion in any way you wish, or arrange the design around the candles you have on hand.

The next step is to mound some dampened spagnum moss or shredded green paper around the candles. Make the mound about 4" deep, and

then nestle the pots or the root ball into the moss. Of course, the moss hides the mechanics and the pots. Don't make the moss too damp, or it will sog through the basket to the table.

For the flowers, use gesneriads in smaller pots, if possible, as they are easier to place for best effect. If you must use a larger plant for better color coordination, it is safe to carefully remove the entire plant from the pot, wrap the root ball in plastic wrap, then nestle it in the same moss for a more pleasing effect. A nice combination is one African violet on each side of the center candle, one or two small *sinningias* on each side of the shorter candles, and a plant or *Codonanthe* "Paula" at each end of the design.

The plant or pots should be tipped slightly to the outside of the basket, for a more graceful look. The moss can be packed around each pot or root ball to hold it in place.

I like to use this combination because the *sinningias* and African violets are so varied in color that it is easy to match or blend the colors with the candles, and *Codonanthe* "Paula" has a white bloom that will complement any color scheme. "Paula" has small leaves close together, and it is in bloom constantly. This plant will give a graduation in size of bloom, foliage and color toward the end of the design.

These are the basics. Now add a few sprigs of fern, laurel or other foliage tucked around the plants to make this a very attractive centerpiece.

This same arrangement, with or without the candles, may be used for a buffet table, coffee table, or anyplace else for viewing both sides of

Completed design

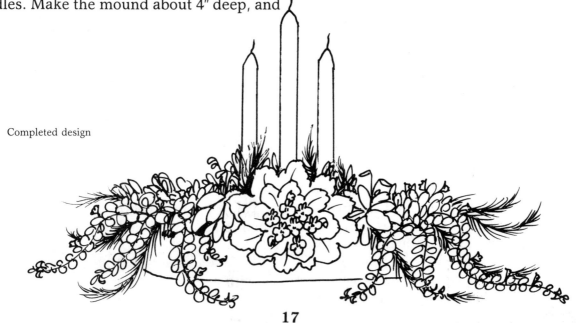

the design. Any number of interesting potted plants may be used in this manner.

As a gift, this is a very nice way to present several plants to someone, for a special occasion. They can use the centerpiece for the occasion itself, and have a "starter" garden of potted plants when the event is over.

A mantle arrangement along these same lines is a nice way to share the joy of bringing these colorful plants into bloom. The only change to make in the original design is to omit the plants on the wall side of the mantle, since they would be hidden from view, anyway.

Holidays are excellent times to use color in plants to complement home decor. My favorite design is to use a long seed tray (a celery tray or other long container would do) and cover it with bright red foil. Secure a fat red candle in the center, and mound the moss around it. Place *aeschynanthus* "Firewheel", which is a beautiful Christmas red, in the tray, along with the green foliage. If blossoms are sparse at this time, add a few red carnations or other cut flowers to bring the color needed, and round out the color scheme. A few loops of red ribbon, or red Christmas ornaments; clusters of holly with red berries, add a festive touch. Gold or silver sparkle will always add a special touch, too.

is "Angel Wing." Trailers lend themselves so well to these designs, because the graceful "trails" may be placed to great advantage, and generally they are very floriferous at all seasons.

Apicias are particulary nice for home decorating. Their colorful foliage varies from deep pebbled green to white, bronze, gold and red varigation; plus all colors of green, silver and pink tones. The range of plant sizes is so varied as to enhance designs from miniature plantings to large-scale exhibits. If *Apicias* are grown as hanging basket plants, the stems may be placed in many positions for greater effect.

Home floral designs need not be large or fancy, or take a lot of time in preparation. A very quick arrangement might be to use a round ceramic ash tray with three miniature *sinningia* plants in a bed of moss. Again, tip the little pots outward to show off the plants. Use a favorite figurine, or a piece of weathered wood for the center of the design to make an interesting arrangement for the coffee table in the living room, or for a breakfast table. This takes a minimum of time and effort, but can add so much to your enjoyment of the plants. Adding dried or treated material to these designs always means extra interest.

Combining dried and treated material with fresh flowers dates back many years to when

If you prefer to use plants, rather than cut flowers, there are many colors of *sinningias*, African violets, *apicias*, *smithiantha*, *columnae* and many more with red, white and pastel color that blend beautifully with Christmas red and green. *Sinningia* "Black Light" is a true bright red; *nematanthus* is also a true red, with extra interest of the pendant-type blossoms. African violet "Cotton Bowl" is a very full double white; an African violet trailer that is a joy to design with

homes did not have forced air heating and cooling. Summer flowers and foliage were dried or treated for winter use, as were the fruits and vegetables for food.

The love of flowers is as old as time itself. Let us not change this time-honored devotion.

Handy Hint: Never place fresh flowers or potted plants on a television set. The heat from the set, when it is on, will cause any fresh material to deteriorate and fade quickly. Also, it is not a good idea to place anything even damp, much less wet, on an electrical appliance of any kind!

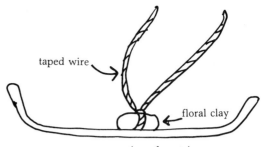

cross section of container

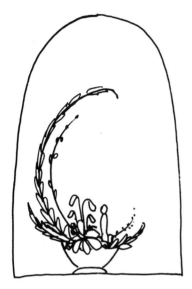

wire to the bottom of the container with a walnut-sized ball of floral clay. Place the wire on the bottom of the container, and place the ball of clay on top, pressing down firmly. Then place a square of floral foam to fit the container on top of the clay, bring the wire around it and twist for a firm hold on the foam. The wire will hold the block of floral foam to the bottom of the container.

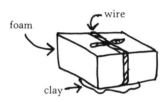

There is a return to the architectural design of many years ago, of building houses with a niche in the entryway, or as part of the hallway design. These niches are particularly nice for a combination arrangement of dried or treated material, with the addition of fresh flowers or plants for special occasions.

These designs take a bit more planning for we must consider the space allowed, or the limited space of a niche, so we can work for a design to the proper scale. A small niche would require a delicate design using small flowers and more delicate foliage. An excellent container for such designs is a Chinese rice bowl or similar container. These may be purchased in plain china or highly decorated and brightly colored. In order to occasionally change the color scheme more easily, I find it best to work with a plain color or white, but it is a matter of choice. Dried arrangements will last many months, so the mechanics must be secure to avoid problems of falling or shifting of material.

Now you are ready to begin the design. Always start at the back of the design for convenience; it is easier to add material toward the front. Grape tendrils are light and airy to use as a design element, but if these are not available, tape

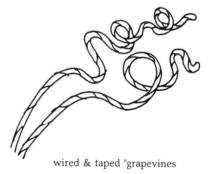

wired & taped "grapevines

A form material that comes in styrofoam-like blocks especially made for dried arrangements is available at floral supply houses, or common floral foam (used dry) will do nicely to hold all the components in proper place. Attach a Florataped

medium wire with straw colored tape. Bend the wire in interesting shapes to give the desired effect of curling and twisting. A crescent shape is a versatile design and when used in a niche with the curve toward the entry, gives a welcome feeling. The green-grey *banksia* foliage has a subtle effect when used with off-white German statice for the center 'filler'. For special occasions add orchid tubes to the design so you can incorporate fresh blossoms.

Grapevine (or raffia or straw) wreath with *aeschynanthus* foliage & *sinningia* blossoms & fern in orchid tubes

Treated or dried materials are used many times to highlight or bring attention to certain parts of an arrangement. Methods of these procedures are covered in another chapter. There is one instance where I would not recommend using 'treated' material and that is a bubble bowl or underwater arrangement. The reason being: treated material will sometimes 'bleed' into the water, or cause it to become 'cloudy', thus detracting from the desired effect.

Rocks, shells, driftwood or any material gathered from the beach, or having been in contact with salt water, must be treated before using in any type of design. The most common treatment for any of these items is to soak overnight in a solution of one cup household ammonia to two gallons of warm water. If the item floats, weigh it down with a heavy object so it stays submerged. When treatment is finished, wash all objects in warm water and dry in strong sunlight if possible. To bleach driftwood, soak overnight in bleach solution of ½-cup bleach to two gallons of water. Remove from solution (do not rinse), place in strong sunlight, turn occasionally to bleach both sides.

Some of the designs being featured in shows currently are Kinetics, the study of motion. Among these are Mobiles, Stabiles, and Stamobiles.

MOBILES – A true mobile should make a complete circle, with ever-changing relationships as the individual parts move independently but in carefully controlled design patterns. The objective in building a mobile is the illusion of objects floating freely in space. Dramatic effects in a mobile may be achieved by the 'near misses' and the space-form relationships as it turns.

STABILES – An image that gives an impression of movement, suggested motion, illusionary kinetics. Weathered wood or driftwood is one of nature's stabiles. Wire sculpture, ceramic statuary, ice sculpture, etc., of animals, birds, or humans may give the feeling of arrested or impending motion. The design itself does not move; one must create line patterns and structural rhythms that urge one to view it from all sides to get the full impact of the design. A stabile must be a free-standing structure that has concealed sources to support the plant material. It can be elevated on a rod or stand to become an airborne sculpture. To be entered in a show a stabile must contain plant material, fresh, dried or treated even if the base material is natural, such as driftwood, weathered wood or such. It is the designer's option to use fresh plant material in such a way as not to diminish the design impact of the stabile.

The STAMOBILE is another step in developing kinetic design – a STABILE with illusionary

movement and the added rhythm of actual movement. The moving parts support the implied movement of the stamobile. Air currents affect the speed and motion, and the different positions determine the design relationships of the forms to the structure.

Some ways to induce movement in stabiles are: use of a spring or piano wire, for up and down action, or nylon fishing line for a twirling or pendulum motion.

Orchid picks are covered with colored florist's tape to simulate butterfly bodies. Blossoms keep fresh in water-filled orchid picks during flower show.

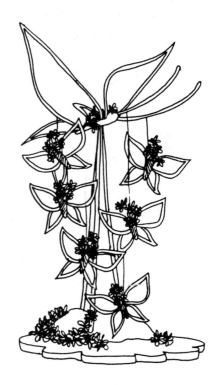

STAMOBILE: bamboo stand, large butterfly. Smaller butterflies hang from fishing line. Butterfly bodies are orchid picks filled with African violet blossoms. African violet blossoms at base of design. Color scheme: white bamboo butterflies, stand, base. Pink blossoms, florist's tape on orchid picks. Darker pink aquarium gravel mounded at base of stand.

An example of a STAMOBILE can be studied in the center color section of this book.

"O.K. — let's do that underwater design!"

UNDERWATER DESIGNS or BUBBLE BOWLS have long been in use by Florists and commercials, but have only been used in shows for the last few years. These unique designs are a pleasure to work with, but have many restrictions; the entire design must be totally underwater. It may be open or closed at the top but no material must extend out of the water. In some shows the rule is that no material shall touch the sides or back of the bowl. They must have a design, conform to the schedule, and generally they will depict movement, which puts them in the field of kinetics. The basic principles and elements of design must be followed in these procedures, but the mechanics are somewhat different. A pin frog, securely fastened to the base, is very important. All plant material, including flowers, must be securely fastened to the pin frog by forcing the end of the stems onto the sharp prongs of the pin frog. Otherwise they will float to the top as soon as water is poured in the container. ALL materials used in these arrangements should be rinsed thoroughly before they are used. This keeps the water clear at all times.

These designs should be kept light and airy-looking, so leave room to look like it has movement, or the illusion of movement. Mechanics must be covered. Small pieces of fern will attach easily to the sharp prongs of the pin frog, also contrasting colors of marbles, colored rocks, gravel, washed sand, etc. are just a few of the ways to camouflage the mechanics. ONE caution: after you have filled the container, be sure to check and see that the force of the water has not disturbed the sand or whatever you have used to cover the base. The best way to fill the container is to use a watering vessel with a spout and pour the water down the side of the container (the inside, of course). Add at least two thirds of the water the night before so everything will settle in place. If it must be moved, it will take less time for any little 'thingies' to either surface or settle to the bottom. It is my considered opinion that living things should not be used in a design, which does include fish or aquatic snails and such. Many plants are toxic to water creatures and cut plant material, or even whole plants, sometimes become deadly to any form of life, and contaminate the whole design. It also causes the water to become cloudy and unattractive.

A suggestion from Dorothy Kahrmann:
To add water to your underwater design, attach a tube to a funnel, so that when water is poured in, it can be directed to the side of the container, leaving the arrangement undisturbed.

DESIGN begins with the space allowed. The center of interest is the heart of the design, also the stability. When it is necessary to use small flowers in a design, they should be unified or clustered to give the illusion of larger blossoms.

The basic principles and elements of design should be followed at all times in any artistic endeavor.

Selecting and preparing your base is of utmost importance. if it is not the color you wish, it is a simple matter to change the tone or entire color in several different ways. A matte or dull finish is generally preferred, as a shiny or high-gloss finish tends to detract from the overall effect. Floral sprays, fermate, soot, shoe polish, Fuller's earth, talcum powder, are just a few of the materials that may be used to obtain the desired effect. A high gloss or shine may be subdued greatly by use of these materials. Use a small amount on a soft cloth or your fingertip, and rub the object gently until the desired tone is achieved. The surplus may be removed with a soft brush. This does not change the color but it tones down the high gloss, which avoids detracting from the overall design.

All entries in arrangement classes must have all mechanics well concealed, otherwise points will be deducted if judges see any part of them. This is from the front or normal viewing point. In most shows the design division is staged with a backdrop, draping or along a wall. Judges are not allowed to touch or pick up a design, so they will be viewed and judged from the same position.

The only exception to this rule is pertaining to kinetics. These designs must show movement and are somewhat viewed from different angles. In some cases a judges chairman will instruct a panel of judges to touch a design to prove its mobility. The same rule as far as concealing mechanics applies to these entries as well.

Background material is usually rigid or doesn't cooperate with the desired curve. A fern frond may be pruned to the desired shape, then laid flat on a table top, with a weight on the stem and a small fish weight attached to the tip. Leave it in this position for several hours, then make a fresh cut on the end of the stem and immerse in plain water for several hours or overnight, keeping the curve secured. This same process may be used on branches of eucalyptus, pussy willow, laurel and others.

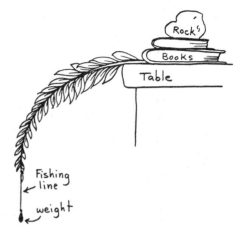

Another way to curve rigid background material is to gently stroke the stem in the direction you wish it to bend. If using branches of ivy, *aeschynanthus*, *nematanthus* or any flexible material, use size 22 wire and starting about 2" from the tip, gently wire the stem in a spiral down to the bottom, and secure with floral tape. It may then be stroked into the desired shape.

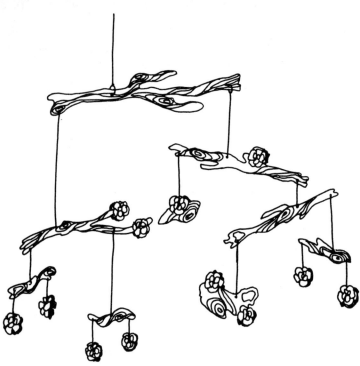

MOBILE: African violet blossoms & driftwood pieces.

Kinetics — Design and Construction

KINETICS: the study of motion. Webster's dictionary goes a bit further and gives this description: of or relating to the motion of material bodies and the forces of energy associated therewith.

The differences from Stabiles, Stamobiles and a Kinetic have been described at the beginning of this chapter, so we will deal with Mobiles and their construction at this point.

A mobile must move with a slight movement of air, therefore it is obvious the most lightweight material must be used. Decide on the design, assemble all material, and this is the time to very carefully check the show schedule, if it is to be entered in a show. If you are doing this for your own pleasure, this is a good way to get in practice. Don't assume your first efforts will automatically be award winners, but work toward that goal.

Many shows furnish open picture frames, all the same size and color, for a better appearance and harmony. If you don't have one the size you need for building a mobile at home, a handy

husband may construct one from material from a frame shop, or 1"x2" lumber. It is not necessary to have these finished and painted unless that is your choice, as these will be used at home, but may be used to transport the mobile to a show.

Some schedules allow dried or treated blossoms and material to be used and for practical purposes I suggest these for the first attempt.

Basic material needed will be invisible thread, or lightweight monofilament fishing line, small clear plastic drinking straws, gesneriad blossoms, fresh or dried; also any foliage if that is part of the design.

You may start at the top or bottom. Actually, each component is balanced individually, so the middle is as good a starting point as any. The important thing to remember is the entire mobile must be able to make a complete turn within the frame without touching any part of it. With a hot needle I punch a small hole in each end of the top plastic straw, then one in the straw about one-third from one end. This will be the one to hold the pilot thread that will hold the mobile to the top of the frame. Tie a section of thread or line

MOBILE CONSTRUCTION:

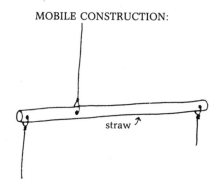

straw ↗

to each end of the straw. Caution: allow plenty of line, for it is easier to trim it off than find you are trying to tie a knot in a line that is too short. Do not have all straws the same length, but make holes in subsequent straws (crossbars) the same as the first one. The first one that I made only used gesneriad blossoms, but as you advance in this art, do get bolder and try more different materials.

A good balance tool is a six-inch section of wooden dowel. Lay the straw across it at the point it is attached to the line. This will tell you which end to attach the heavy part of the next section. Do not make a permanent tie in the top end of the line until the entire mobile is balanced. This is why you need extra line to pull up or let out

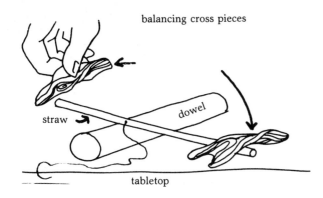

balancing cross pieces

straw

dowel

tabletop

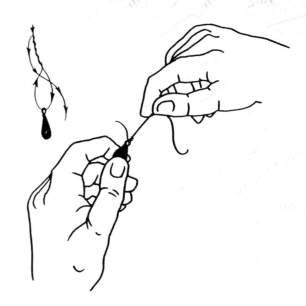

for balance in each step. Tie a loop in the bottom end of line about the size of a dime. Attach two blossoms back to back (African violet blossoms are easy to do), over the loop and secure with a small amount of glue. Do this same procedure for all

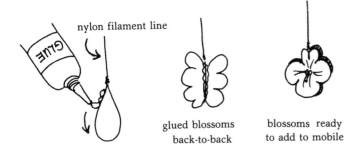

nylon filament line

GLUE

glued blossoms back-to-back

blossoms ready to add to mobile

The SNELL TIE LOOP for hanging blossoms on a mobile:

blossoms to be used in the mobile. Thread the line through the straw in the top crossbar, taking up or letting out on the line until it is in balance. Once you get the first bar balanced, the rest is easy. As you finish each step, check to see that it will make a complete turn.

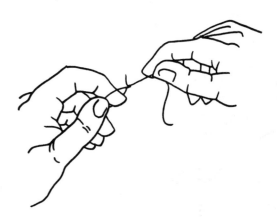

1. First, start to make a snell tie, but do *not* pull knot tight. Place finger or thumb *in* loop and draw down to desired size.
2. Pull knot tight in that spot to produce desired loop.

The SNELL TIE for tying snug: use to attach fishing weights to branches, etc.

1. Arrows indicate direction the end of fishing line should be travelling as the knot is fashioned.

2. Wrap line 5 times around itself.

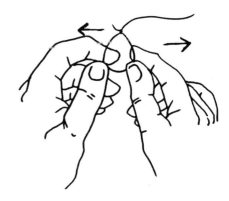

3. Tug on loop from sides to "set" knot firmly.
4. Loop is now ready to use in mobile.

25

After your first success you will want to experiment further with other materials. A hike on the beach will glean a wealth of pencil-size driftwood in many interesting shapes. Small shells and dried seaweed can send your creative senses reeling with all the possible designs. A pin-sized drill will make an almost invisible hole for the line to go through.

Margaret Waguespack, award-winning designer, has sent some good suggestions on this subject. With her permission, I quote:

"Some arrangers will use only featherweight material; in fact, some actually use feathers. There is nothing wrong with using feathers. I have seen them used beautifully. Do use them in an original manner.

"It is sometimes more difficult to use heavier material successfully, yet doing so is a challenge and may produce a striking effect. There is no rule that says a mobile most flutter like a moth. if you use depth and balance properly, movement should follow.

"The kind of flowers and foliage you use may mean the difference between a blue ribbon and a lesser award. I am not referring to color here. Use blossoms with heavy substance and strong stems and check them out for endurance before the show. Containers on mobiles will be minute in order to keep the arrangements actually moving and will hold little water. The constant movement tends to dry them out, also. If you are allowed to do so, replenish the water supply and the blooms the morning before judging. Thicker foliage holds up better than thin. Some gesneriads I recommend are *aeschynanthus* and *Columnea* for blooms—the heavier the substance of the flower, the better.

"Nowhere in design is planning ahead more important than in the class for mobiles. Be certain you will have plenty of blossoms for replacements. The amount of flowering material in a mobile is usually sparse, therefore it will appear especially prominent. Remember, too, that there are many shades and hues of a chosen color. For example, there is blush pink, rose pink, coral pink, and so on. Choose the particular color that is just right for the effect you want.

"Do not blithely assume that you will be able to find just the right color(s) you need. Whether the show is across town or across the country, you will avoid last-minute panic and/or having to use colors that are not quite right, by taking along the parent plant. If this is not possible, then plan to arrive a day early and search out a grower or nursery. Believe me, variations in color can make an enormous difference in the picture you are trying to project.

"In any type of hanging arrangement, I believe contrast between the background and moving materials is very important. This allows you to decide where the emphasis should be—and this is transmitted to the onlooker (and to the judges if you are successful). I like to use light colors for the material in the mobile—and a very dark background. Or the reverse, dark on light.

"Unless you are a genius at this sort of thing, you must do a lot of experimenting. Try adding a few of the moving parts at a time. This way, you won't become frustrated and develop a "to h--- with it" attitude.

"More than any other type of arrangement, a mobile must be planned long before the show—not only planned, in fact, but assembled. My husband ducked the skeleton of a mobile for weeks (it was suspended from a hanging lamp). Not only do you need to give your creation a trial flight, there can be other problems. If you have never tried tieing knots in nylon fishing line or its equivalent, let old fumble-fingers warn you, it is not a job to save till the last minute."

Printed with the kind permission of Mrs. Margaret Waguespack, Editor of The Dixie News, official publication of the Dixie African Violet Society, encompassing Alabama, Louisiana, Florida, Texas, Georgia, Mississippi, North and South Carolina and Arkansas. For more information about The Dixie African Violet Society contact Mrs. Waguespack at 334 Halsey Dr., Harahan, LA 70123.

"Hold it! That's exactly the effect I wanted!"

CHAPTER III

TOOLS:

container for submerging leaves
shells
rocks
driftwood
pin frog
marbles
colored rocks
gravel
washed sand
water vessel with spout or funnel
soft brush
small fishing weights
practice frame
darning needle or ice pick
votive candle or cigarette lighter
6″ piece of 1″ dowel (or equivalent)
hobby pin-sized drill
wire cutter or heavy-duty scissors
bird-nosed pliers

SUPPLIES

invisible thread or monofilament fishing line
small clear plastic drinking straws
trout swivels
white craft glue
piano wire or 24-gauge wire
blossoms, fresh or dried
pencil-sized driftwood
small shells
feathers
dried plant material
garden greenery for practice
household ammonia*
household bleach*
florist's clay
floral spray
talcum powder
fermate
monofilament fishing line
floral tape

NEVER mix ammonia with bleach: it produces hydrochloric gas, which is very deadly!

Wedding bouquet of *aeschynanthus* foliage and blossoms, *sinningia* leaves, fern & taped wire "grapevines."

CHAPTER IV

Body Flowers

Techniques and Suggestions for Use

Body flowers are corsages, wristlets, Colonial (or nosegay), hairpieces, presentation bouquets and many other ways of wearing or carrying flowers. This is the general definition of body flowers.

The delicate texture of most gesneriad blossoms make them very adaptable to dainty, light weight corsages, hairpieces, etc. The most important thing to remember in making these designs is to keep them light in weight. If using larger flowers it is wise to take them apart and reassemble the petals. This procedure is known as feathering, or Frenching.

Large corsages are heavy and if worn on sheer material, they are very unattractive, and cause the garment to look ill-fitting and uncomfortable. No one wants to appear at a social affair looking like they had just come in first in the fifth race at Santa Anita.

Wiring and taping these blossoms require different types of procedures. The rosette form should be wired with the hook method, and the tubular form should have the hairpin method. Both of these procedures are described on the following page.

All plant material should be pre-conditioned. This is done by making a fresh cut in the stem end, submerging the cut part in at least two inches of tepid water. A few hours will do nicely, but it is better if they can be conditioned overnight. Do not let blossoms rest in water as they may become soft and discolored. Some leaves and branches may be totally submerged in water overnight and benefit greatly. This is a matter for experimenting, as water in most metropolitan areas differ a great deal, so the best method is experiment.

Mature leaves of *Nemanthus* 'Bijou', *aeschynanthus* 'Black Pagoda', *Episcia, Smithianthia,* African violet and many other gesneriad leaves are very striking in corsages, also all types of wedding designs. Some of them are more colorful on the back; so they may be used to highlight or tone down colors and textures.

When this plant material has been conditioned it becomes very turgid and breaks easily. I would suggest practicing the procedures on several of the same type blossoms before starting the design.

If you are using net and ribbon, these should be wired and taped in advance. The leaves or background material should also be prepared. (For detailed instructions on these procedures, see last page of this chapter.) The blossoms should be wired last as the warmth of the hands tends to soften the stem. The final assembly should be done with as little handling as possible. A box or plastic container with a small amount of shredded wax paper or a facial tissue on the bottom works well to protect the delicate blossoms and help preserve the originality of the design. This should be prepared in advance of the time it is to be used.

There is an old saying in the Florist industry, "When presenting flowers to anyone, always give them a kiss." I don't know where this custom originated, but a lot of people are having fun, so let's not spoil a good thing.

All corsages should have two corsage pins, hairpieces should have two bobby pins or combs. In other words, they should have two places of attachment. The reason: it is very difficult to attach anything being worn with only one fastener. Invariably it will 'flop' or hang crooked, and be very uncomfortable. This tends to spoil the effect of a lovely intention.

Corsages and hair decorations should be well-anchored with more than one pin or hairpin!

Boutonnieres for men usually require only one pin, because of their size. A common fantasy of some ladies is that men hesitate to wear a boutonniere. I can assure you that in many years as a wedding designer, I have never encountered a man who hesitated to have his lapel properly pinned. I have given many programs to men's clubs on the proper way to present and pin corsages and boutonnieres. Men are equally interested in flowers and their culture. If you doubt this statement, just look around at the next club meeting or show.

We have a husband/wife team in one of the

clubs of which I am a member. They enter in the horticulture in competition, but the fun begins when they both enter the same classes in the design division. This has been going on for several years and they are still happily married. Which proves a good point—we can compete with our best friend and whoever wins, we are still friends.

Creating Unusual
Body Flower Corsages

During the nine years (1960-1969) I owned and operated the Golden Orchid Flower Shop in Santa Cruz, California, my main corsage work was with species orchids. Most design schools do not work much with orchids, because they are expensive; as a result, many fine designers are timid about using orchids and other delicate-looking flowers.

At one point, in a fit of madness, I accepted a challenge and $50 wager from a fashion designer, who said that I could not, on short notice, design a different orchid corsage for any outfit. So, during an actual fashion show, I stood by to whip up corsage designs.

Of course, he knew what was coming, but I only learned a few minutes before the model was to appear what she was wearing. You should have seen the smirk on his face when the first girl came out in a bikini! In desperation, I whipped up a tiny "belly-button" corsage made with *epidendrums* and *laeliacattleya* wired to a tiny piece of net in the back. The net was sprayed with floral glue to hold it in place on the girl's body.

The next model also wore a bikini, so to do something different, I fashioned a "big toe corsage."

This frantic bit of creativity not only won the bet for me, but led to work for the 3M company, gluing orchids on scarves, veils and people for displays and shows.

This adventure was written up by *The Florists' Review* (March 30, 1972) as part of a biographical article on The Golden Orchid shop and my designs.

Later, acting as staging chairman for the "Miss California" pageant in Santa Cruz, the "belly-button" and "big toe" corsages were used to good effect in showing how flowers can be worn with *any* outfit.

Similar tiny corsages could be made with

gesneriads: one might use *Achimenes, Sinningia,* African violets or *Koellikeria Erinoides,* or any number of other interesting blossoms. A very tiny corsage is made exactly like a larger one, just scaled down.

BODY FLOWERS can include: hair decorations, mini-nosegay on the finger, wrist corsage, belly-button corsage, toe corsage.

How to Make Professional
Florists' Bows

A professional bow is made the same way, whether it is made from ¼" corsage ribbon or 5" wide ribbon for potted plants or church aisle decoration. Start by holding the ribbon about 5" from the end in a firm grip between thumb and forefinger. Hold the ribbon with the dull (not shiny) or unprinted side *up* and with the other hand bring the ribbon firmly over the thumb; this forms the appearance of a "knot" for the bow, though it never really becomes a knot at all. Then give the ribbon a twist while it passes under the thumb, so the satiny or printed side of the ribbon is now up. Make a short loop of ribbon on both sides of the "knot" (which remains over the thumb for the entire making of the bow), twisting the ribbon between thumb and forefinger each time, so the "good" side is up.

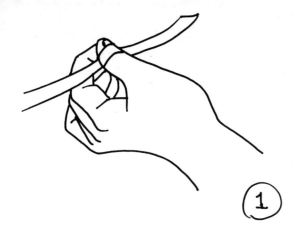

For a small bow, these first two loops should be only about ½" or so; for larger bows, use your judgement about making a couple of short loops on either side of the "knot" for starters. These short loops serve the purpose of filling in the space between the "knot" and the rest of the bow. After these first two loops, make the rest of the loops as large as you wish for the finished bow, each time giving the ribbon a twist between

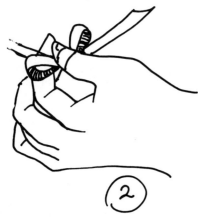

thumb and forefinger so the best side of the ribbon is always in view. The average florist's bow has at least 9 loops on each side of the "knot" but you may wish to make an even fuller bow. A small 4" wide bow will take at least 1½ yards of ribbon; a larger bow may take several yards more.

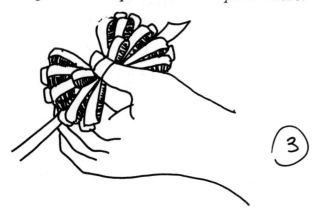

When the bow is the desired size, clip the ribbon off opposite to the 5" piece which started the bow. *Do not let go of the bow with thumb and forefinger or it will fall apart!* Take a 6" piece of #28 bare florist's wire and carefully slide it underneath the "knot" over the thumbnail. Do this gently, so as not to damage the ribbon or catch yourself with

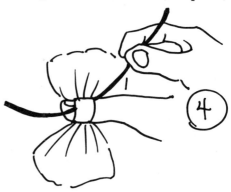

the wire. This cautious reminder will be unnecessary after you have run the wire under your nail a few times. *Then* you get *real* careful. Now gently but firmly pull the wire down around the thumb until the wire is underneath the bow. Twist the wire very firmly as close to the ribbon as possible for three or four twists. The tighter the wire is twisted under the bow, the more control

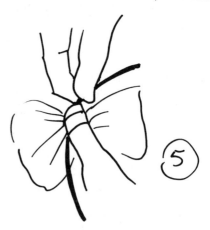

you will have in arranging the loops of ribbon. Do not let go of the bow until the wire has been twisted tightly against the ribbon several times. Now remove the thumb and forefinger from the completed bow, fluff out the loops, and you have a professional bow!

The florist's secret for perfectly beautiful bows: NEVER *tie* a bow to anything; always wire it to corsages, or to a wooden pick for placement in a design or potted plant.

(very light pink, white, pearl, spring green, etc.) unless a special effect is desired. Several colors may be used in a "round" pouf to achieve a particular color.

Poufs may be made any size, for a fluffy or especially cute effect in a design, but should not be overpowering in a corsage.

MAKING A BOW: 1. Form "knot" over thumb; 2. Make ½" beginning loops; 3. Continue with larger loops; 4. Slide wire under "knot" carefully; 5. Pull knot underneath bow and twist firmly around all the loops in back of bow; 6. Fluff out your perfect bow!

Professional Poufs for Corsages

This very simple addition to corsages helps add fullness, fill in where something light and airy is needed, and also protects the delicate flowers from contact and possible damage with the corsage foliage or even the wearer's skin. Poufs can be made larger to wire onto wooden picks for potted plants or designs, but should be used with discretion.

A pouf for a corsage is simply a 2"x5" piece of very fine net, gathered by the fingers and caught with a 6" piece of #28 bare wire. One piece of net makes a "flat" pouf and more than one piece of net will make a "round" or fluffy pouf when pulled out around the wire.

The best colors for poufs are subtle shades

Florists' "Mouse Ears" for Corsages

"Mouse ears" are small loops of ribbon added to corsages to protect the delicate flowers from inadvertantly brushing against the corsage when wearing it, and from makeup. "Mouse ears" are also good for a bit of color where needed, and for filling in small spaces. Though originally designed for corsages, "mouse ears" can also be used in a design, where needed.

"Mouse ears" are made with one loop of ribbon, made to the size desired. A "tail" is left sticking up, usually, as shown. This loop and tail is wired firmly, and covered with the same color florists' tape being used for the rest of the corsage. More than one loop of ribbon may be used in a "mouse ear" but discretion should be used; these little bits of color should be a subtle addition to the corsage or design.

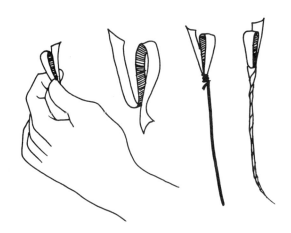

MAKING "MOUSE EARS": 1. Form loop with ribbon; 2. Clip ribbon so one end sticks up; 3. Place wire in loop, twist firmly; 4. Tape down "mouse ear" to end of wire.

flat pouf   round pouf

MAKING A "POUF": 1. Gather "pouf" net with fingers; 2. Twist wire in middle of net to form "pouf".

33

Wiring a Branch of Foliage

Whether wiring a tiny branch of leafy foliage for a corsage, or a large branch for a design, the principle is the same. Lay a 10" piece of covered wire close along the stem up to the first or second branching of leaves, and bend the wire carefully around the main stem once. The wire used should be covered, either the standard covered florists' wire or use florists' tape of the desired color, as some of the wire will be up above the taping of the stem. Bend the wire only once around the stem, between branching leaves, to hold it firmly. Without damaging the stem or leaves, bend the wire as closely to the stem as possible so that it does not show any more than necessary. Now bring wire back down the stem, and tape the stem and wire together firmly.

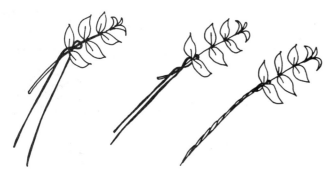

WIRING FOLIAGE: 1. Loop wire over lowest branching of foliage; 2. Twist wire firmly, avoiding lumps; 3. Tape foliage and wire firmly.

Wiring Large Flat Leaves

Make a 10" hairpin shape of #28 covered wire. For large leaves, you may need more wire. Remember it is easier to cut wire off than add on. Push the hairpin of wire through the front of the leaf, about halfway up from the stem. Turn leaf over, and gently pinch the wire down on either side of the leaf. *Do not twist wire;* just lay it alongside the leaf. Wire should be longer than the real stem. Tape the stem and the wire, to the end of the wire. This will give you enough flexibility to gently bend the leaf in whatever direction is

desired (don't worry if you break the real stem; the wire will hold the leaf firmly in place.)

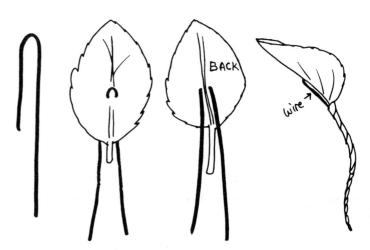

WIRING LARGE FLAT LEAVES: 1. Make "hairpin" of wire, and push through front side of leaf; 2. Bring wire down either side of stem (wire does not have to be even); 3. Pinch wire closer, if needed, to stem; 4. Tape wire and stem.

Wiring Flowers With a Large Calyx

Use a 10" piece of #28 bare wire, and push the wire through the calyx about 1/3 of the way from the stem, leaving 2/3 of the calyx above the wire. Using thumb and forefinger, pinch both wires straight down on either side of the calyx. Using florists' tape, start at point where wire penetrates the calyx, and tape all the way down the wire. it is not necessary to twist the wire around the stem of the flower, and will in fact give a "lumpy" appearance to the wired stem. Continue taping past the real stem to the end of the wires, which will form the corsage "stem".

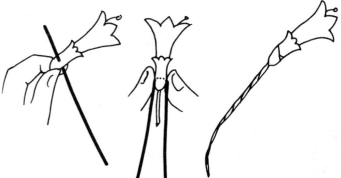

34

WIRING LARGE-CALYX FLOWERS: 1. Place wire through calyx; 2. Press wire down by pinching calyx between fingers; 3. Tape firmly, starting mid-calyx.

type of blossom, it is always worth a try.

With the long, wire "stem" flowers can be gently (VERY gently!) bent to look forward, to take any shape desired.

Wiring Delicate Flowers

Using bare #28 wire, cut a 10" long piece for *each* blossom. Even for bunched flowers, wire each blossom separately. In a design or arrangement where nobody will touch the flowers, a wire can just be stuck into each flower from the bottom of the bud section, and the wire will rest against the stem of the blossom. Tape it a few inches up the stem and place it in the design. However, a "hook" is needed in the wire for a corsage, so the wearer will not get stuck in the face.

Bend a ½" hook in the end of the wire, insert straight end down, through blossom. This should bring wire along the stem. Gently pull the wire from underneath, until the hook "sets" into the flower. *DO NOT TRY TO TWIST THE WIRE.* Catch the wire and stem together with florists' tape, and gently tape down the stem, completely down the wire to form a longer, more flexible "stem".

Use flower buds; they add interest and help graduate the scale of the design or corsage.

If a blossom breaks off the wire, or off its stem, while taping it, just add another wire on the other side of the flower and retape. This may not always work, but if you are short of a particular color or

How to Hold the Florists' Tape

It is best to use the florist's tape properly, and the beginner should start using it correctly now. Since florist's tape is waxed and therefore sticky, if it is allowed to unroll all over your worktable, it will pick up dust and particles of stuff. Therefore you should learn to hold the roll over the little finger of the hand not doing the wrapping, with the tape coming off the roll from the lower edge. Then it will be handy any time it is needed, but will be out of the way and not impede the work.

Place the end of the tape at the back of the stem or flower. Hold the item being taped in one hand and grip the end of the tape firmly, so it will not slip off the flower or stem as you start to wind

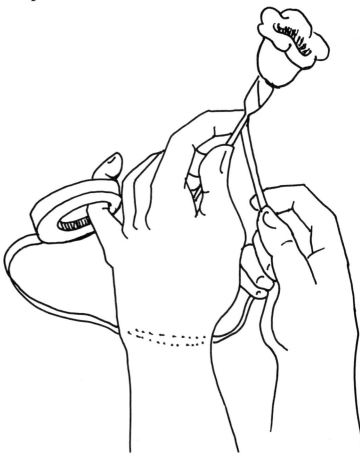

With practice, holding florist's tape to wind it around flower stems will be easy!

WIRING DELICATE FLOWERS: 1. ½" hook; 2. Pull hook down through blossoms; 3. Back of flower; 4. Tape.

35

it. Pull the tape gently to stretch it a bit (remember it is waxed crepe paper and has quite a bit of stretch before it breaks) then, holding the stem and tape firmly, turn the stem counterclockwise, while stretching the tape tightly in a spiral

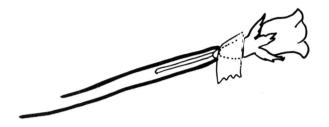

clockwise movement. The tape should also be wound down the stem or wire as this is being done. The sticky tape will stick to itself, and hold to the stem or wire in a firm seal. Lap the edges as you wrap the tape down the stem, so it will completely cover the stem. In this manner, the florist's tape will move off the roll as needed, and not hinder the design in any way.

Beginners need some practice to really master this technique. Make a few "trial runs" of taping to the end of a piece of wire or stem, to learn how to tape smoothly down a stem without leaving "chicken legs" or lumps. Also learn how to judge about how long a stem you'll need for a corsage or design; an eighteen inch stem for a corsage is a bit wasteful of time and material.

"CHICKEN LEG" TAPING

Tape should be pressed gently against the flower or foliage at top point, with starting flap *down,* to hide the torn end. Then wrap tape firmly but gently around the area to be taped, and start a spiral down the stem. Florists' tape will stick to itself, and can be pulled gently as it is wrapped, to make a smooth "stem."

When using a wire as part of a stem, or adding wire to achieve more flexibility, tape down the wire to the entire end and cut squarely across the wire. This gives the wire a blunt end, instead of a sharp pointed end. The tape can then be pulled over the end of the wire, and pressed gently to cover it safely. This is very important when constructing a corsage for someone to wear. There should never be any points sticking out of a corsage.

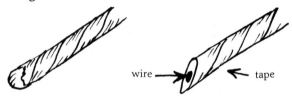

Taped wire for corsage: Taped and cut wire for placing
                                              in design:

wire   tape

My recommendation for florist's tape is Floratape, manufactured by American Can Company. They produce a quality product that I used for years in my florist shop. Floratape comes in sixteen different colors, many of which would be useful to amateur floral designers. Though florist's tape in light green, medium green or olive are the most popular colors for standard use, Floratape currently offers: white and ivory for wedding bouquets, straw color for use with dried materials, mint-ivory for when a shade between white and green is needed; brown and the brownish twig green are useful on branches, stems and for natural wood-like effects; black for boutonnieres or for corsages to be worn against black or for modern designs; pink and orchid are nice with dainty corsages or bouquets; red for holidays. Floratape also has light blue and yellow, plus purple and orange tape for exotic designs or crafts work. Floral supply houses may have the Floratape "Rainbow Pack" with the first fourteen colors listed above.

A method of using orchid tubes with strong wires to produce a "tree" or other structure on which to display blooms is shown here. The same method can be used to create a wire "stem" for short-stemmed blossoms, and to also place them anywhere you wish them, in your design. Shown here are two methods of taping the wires onto the tubes, for maximum display of the blooms, and to accomodate whatever design you have in mind. When the tube and wire are taped correctly, it will not be obvious to the observer.

Attach a wire to the orchid tube by twisting a size #22 wire around the tube top with a tight twist to hold it secure. A moss green Floratape is used to tape the tube to cover it. Do not tape the wire to the orchid tube, as it must be free to be moved in different positions as the fresh flower is inserted in the water-filled tube (as shown).

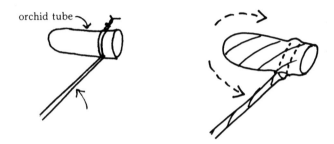

orchid tube

"Moveable" orchid tube—
(1) Twist wire around the top of orchid tube—

(2) Tape tube, *then* down wire—this allows tube to be turned in any direction, by swiveling on the wire.

Most any color of fresh blossom will be attractive in this neutral background. Then tape the wire to a point, so it will be easy to insert into the dry foam base. The wired tubes may be removed, filled with water and a fresh flower, inserted in the floral foam at an appealing angle for an attractive arrangement. When the fresh flowers fade they may be removed and replaced, while the remainder of the design is intact to be used again with may be a different color or type of flower.

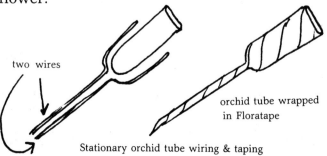

two wires

orchid tube wrapped in Floratape

Stationary orchid tube wiring & taping

Make a "tree" of orchid tubes

Place "tree" in a gift plant

Leaves to be used in a design can be shaped any way you wish to produce the type and size of leaf desired, if you are using a sturdy leaf that will not wilt. Leaves can be wired and taped, then bent slightly, or added to a branch, or manipulated in various ways.

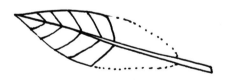

Trim large leaf to make any sized leaf needed for design or corsage.

To make a small leaf from a larger one, cut away the bottom part of the leaf, leaving a small spine. When it is trimmed as desired, wire the leaf and tape it.

THE PERFECT CORSAGE: 1. Main or focal flower, 2. Secondary focus, 3. Tertiary focus, 4. & 5. Additional color, 6. A bud to add balance to the design. Background may be all greenery, or a mixture of foliage, poufs and mouse ears. Note that bow is not a static design at bottom of corsage, but shows at different balance points of the design.

Corsage Assembly

With all the components of the corsage already made, including the bow, poufs, "mouse ears", taped foliage and flowers, you are now ready to assemble the finished corsage.

The florists' tape will stick together if pressed firmly, so you can take different components and press them as you wish, to see how they will look together. Even professionals make a practice corsage first when working with very delicate materials, so they have a design "pattern" from which to work.

It is also acceptable, for most uses, to find several favorite corsage basic designs and use them for all your corsage work.

Remember that *EACH STEP MUST BE TAPED AS YOU GO.* If a corsage is pressed together, and taped as a unit, pieces of it can fall out while the corsage is being worn.

Start with a piece of background foliage, and add a flower. Tape these two pieces together. Add a flat pouf for lightness, and tape. Add more foliage, and tape. Add another pouf, perhaps a round, and tape. Add more flowers, and tape. Add "mouse ears" where needed and tape. Each time something is added, hold the corsage up for a good look at the design.

Make sure that all blossoms are NOT pointed in the same direction; bend some gently to make a more pleasant design.

If the foliage needs to be rearranged, leaves can be tucked behind poufs, or "mouse ears" for a more fluid design. Some leaves should be held back in this manner, to give the corsage depth, and not interfere with the flowers.

Do not place two flowers exactly opposite each other; this makes a design look static and uninteresting. Always stagger the placement of the flowers and buds.

When the corsage is completed to your satisfaction, add the bow. Pull the wire up snug, give it several twists (so that the bow does not wobble) and tape it to the main "stem" of the corsage.

Now trim off the excess "stem" or twist it into a curlique for part of the decoration, depending on the design of the corsage. Add two corsage pins, and place corsage in a pretty box or florists' bag.

If a balance is desired for the corsage, a second, smaller corsage may be constructed and added upside-down to the main corsage "stem" with tape. Follow all instructions for making and assembling a corsage to make this "balance" and add it to the main corsage. This balance is not always necessary, but often can be an extra added attraction to the corsage. Use your own judgement; after some practice you will be able to see whether an additional group of flowers, ribbon, poufs and foliage is truly a "balance" or an overweight extraneous glob of unnecessary flowers.

Everyone loves to get a surplus corsage, so even your practice work will not be wasted.

ASSEMBLY OF CORSAGE: 1. A piece of foliage, a flower; 2. Add a flat pouf; 3. Two more flowers, a round pouf; 4. Add more foliage, etc; 5. Completed corsage, with full complement of foliage, poufs, mouse ears, flowers, large bow and corsage pins.

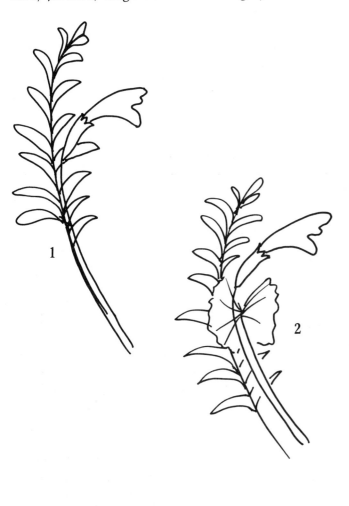

Handy Hints for Corsage-Making

It is easier to cut wire shorter after the taping is done, than to add on to a too-short wire!

Leaves are usually background to the blossom's focal point, but an attractive corsage may be made of greenery alone.

When wiring and taping flowers or leaves, do not twist the wire any more than necessary. Leave the wires as straight as possible down the real stem of the flower or foliage, and tape it slightly around the calyx of the flower, or the stem of the foliage. Continue taping down the stem, past it, and on down the length of the wire. This, then, forms the "stem" to be used in constructing the corsage. Too many twists in the stem-wire will result in a "lumpy" or "chicken-leg" appearance to the "stem."

Wire and tape all greenery before starting on the flowers. Have everything laid out on a towel or cloth, ready to use.

Keep a small hand towel in your lap for frequent wiping of hands while making a corsage.

Condition extra flowers, in case some wilt or

just don't look that good, when corsage-making time comes.

Man-made satin or velvet leaves may be used instead of real leaves, and are easier for the beginner to handle. These leaves can make a corsage look just as professional as using real leaves. Sometimes more so.

For conditioning plants, have a container that will not allow the blossoms to become wet; a pie pan of tepid water is good. To keep blossoms out of water, place a few pieces of *Springeri* fern or any large pieces of sponge rock, or anything that will let the stems of blossoms and foliage stay in water but keep the delicate material from becoming discolored. Have a container ready as you cut the flowers and foliage, to put the stems in water the minute they are cut.

PRACTICE, PRACTICE, PRACTICE! Make up a corsage for your bank teller, babysitter, the little old lady down the block, or some deserving secretary while you are learning the art of corsage-making!

Some foliage used for gesneriad corsages are cuttings that can be started as new plants; an extra surprise for the corsage recipient!

Foliage and poufs are used in a corsage not only for color but to protect delicate flowers from the face and makeup of the wearer; the flowers should always be placed in a corsage so that they will not be damaged by the wearer.

It's really nice to make corsages for a club installation if you have a spouse who brings you coffee or a drink while you're hard at work!

Seven deep purple "Plum Frosty" double African violets are accented with reddish-purple-edged **nematanthus** *"Butterscotch" foliage, and a deep purple ribbon. This corsage symbolized the "loyalty" of a hard-working and dutiful Vice-President.*

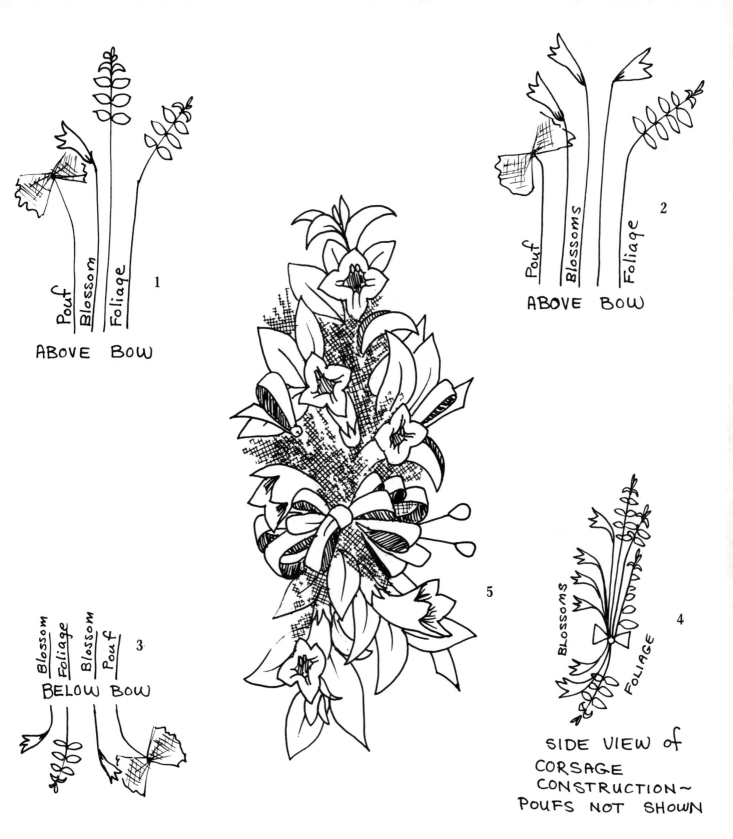

ABOVE BOW

Pouf Blossom Foliage

1

ABOVE BOW

Pouf Blossoms Foliage

2

BELOW BOW

Blossom Foliage Blossom Pouf

3

5

Blossoms Foliage

4

SIDE VIEW of
CORSAGE
CONSTRUCTION~
POUFS NOT SHOWN

*A corsage design with bright red-orange, red-throated **aeschynanthus** "Firewheel" blooms and foliage, utilizing flowers above and below the scarlet bow. This corsage design was used in the installation ceremony of the Bakersfield Off-Shoots Gesneriad Society, awarded to the incoming President to represent the "courage" necessary to be a leader.*

41

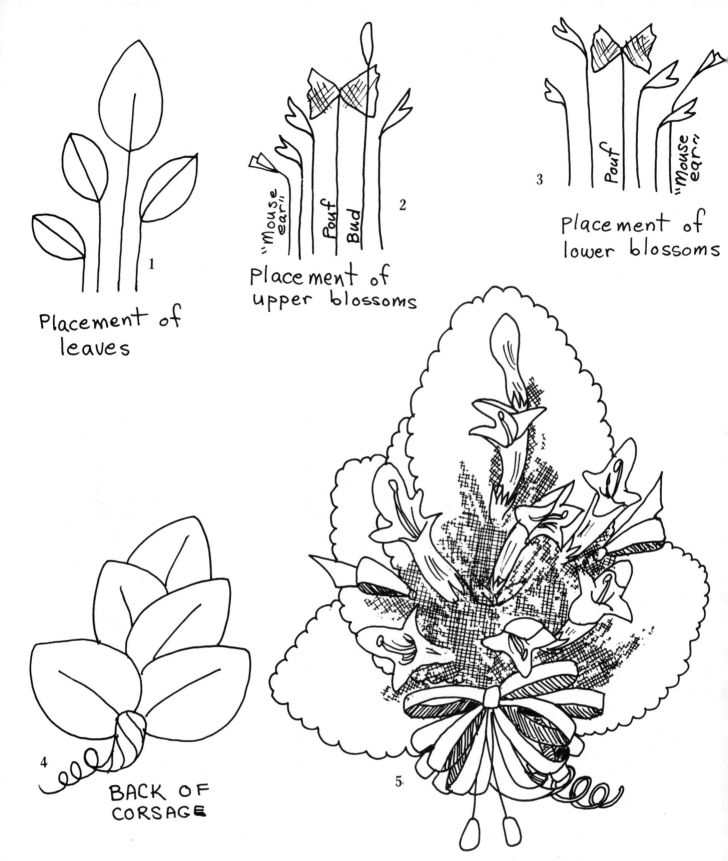

Placement of
leaves

1

Placement of
upper blossoms

"Mouse ear"
Pouf
Bud

2

Placement of
lower blossoms

Pouf
"Mouse ear"

3

4

BACK OF
CORSAGE

5

*A corsage design utilizing red-orange **nematanthus** "Bonfire" blooms and foliage with light-and-dark green **episcia** "Smoky Emerald" leaves. A few **apicia** "Annette" leaves lighten the design. This was accented with a golden yellow bow to represent "fairness" and "honesty" needed to be a club Secretary.*

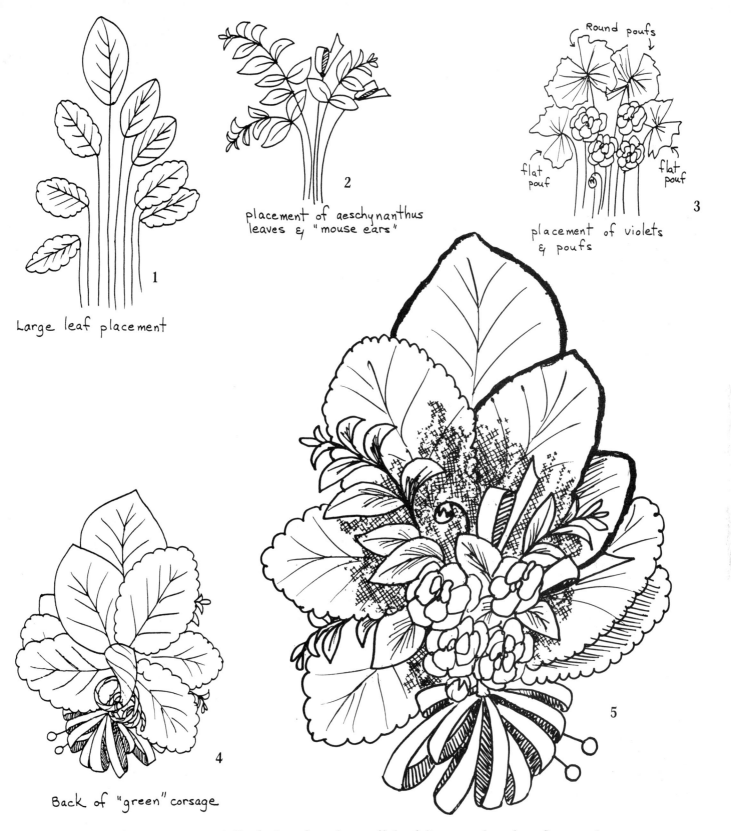

1
Large leaf placement

2
placement of aeschynanthus
leaves & "mouse ears"

3
Round poufs
flat pouf
flat pouf
placement of violets
& poufs

4
Back of "green" corsage

5

A corsage especially designed to show off the foliage, rather than flowers: large velvety **sinningia regina** *leaves layered with reddish-tinted* **Episcia** *"Annette" leaves to form the background for* **aeschynanthus purpossi** *variegated foliage. A few light pink "Trailalong" African violet blossoms add interest. Corsage is tied with a Spring green ribbon almost the same color as the* **aeschynanthus**, *awarded to the incoming Treasurer to represent "endurance" and "patience" required to hold the office.*

Nematanthus "Stoplight"

CHAPTER V

Artistic Plantings (Temporary)

My concept of ARTISTIC PLANTINGS is they belong in TWO different categories. The reason for this is that I believe the temporary planting is designed and constructed specifically for a show or special event. These plantings are not constructed to be a permanent planting, but a temporary arrangement of growing material.

Artistic plantings in this class are those designated with one or more blooming gesneriads (may be removed from the pot) used in an artistic and pleasing manner. These designs are constructed on a base or low container for temporary display. A shallow tray with sand or colorful gravel is very effective in creating these plantings. Do not confuse these with dish gardens or terrariums, etc., which are considered permanent plantings.

All artistic plantings must have a design, so the same principles and elements of design should be followed. Cut plant material may be used, but it should be a minimum amount, and used in such a way to look as if it were growing. Most show schedules will permit line or background material such as: weathered wood, pussy willow branches, rocks, lichen, baby eucalyptus, etc. These items must be used in minimum amounts and arranged in such a pattern as to enhance the design rather than overpower the design. A more natural look may be attained by removing the plant from the pot, covering the root ball with lightweight plastic, then covering the plastic with long fiber spagnum moss. The moss is easier to handle if it is pre-moistened.

Moss may be moistened by pouring hot water

over it in a container. If it is in a plastic bag, cut one corner for a hole large enough to put the hot water in the bag, close the opening, and shake the bag several times, then let it set for five minutes.

Make a wad of moss to tip plant forward,
bury root ball in spagnum moss

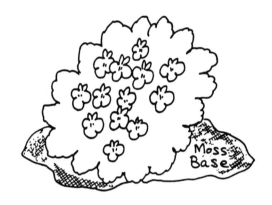

Violet tipped to show off color better

No cut blossoms are allowed in these designs, so this is a place to use those seedlings that you just couldn't bear to part with. Seedlings are grown from seed. They may be a cross-pollination of two of your favorite plants, and if you are lucky you will have a seed pod form on the parent plant. It takes about a year to have a blooming plant from the time of pollination – the ripening of the seed pod, sowing the seed, germinating and growing the seedlings to blooming size. If you wish to name and register these plants, they must be grown through three generations to assure they will grow and bloom true to the seedling parent that has been selected. Many shows have a class for seedlings, but otherwise they cannot be entered in the regular horticultural classes. Seed may be bought from many commercial growers that are advertised in flower magazines and catalogs. More

than one blooming plant is allowed in this class, so cluster the seedlings for a mass of color in the focal point.

Plants themselves are not judged for horticultural perfection as strictly in this class, but condition and the overall impact of the arrangement is very important. When being judged, these designs receive the most points for design and placement of material. They must have a design.

When the base or container is prepared, the line material should be the first portion of the design. Shape the line material and place it at the back of the design. It is better to work from back to front so as not to dislodge any part of the design already placed. If filler material is to be used, now is the time to put it firmly in place. Blooming plants or cut flowers may be placed last to prevent bruising or broken materials.

Using Florist's Tape

Don't be afraid to wire and tape any kind of flowers or foliage. One of the Floratape "Floral Design Pointers"[1] suggests adding tiny tips of pussywillow, small heads of dried grass, holly leaves (with sharp points trimmed away), and even small tips of evergreen to make a corsage more appropriate for the season or occasion.

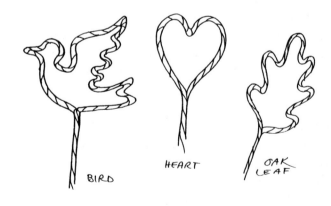

Making wired & taped shapes for corsages, bouquets & designs

[1]"Floral Design Pointers" written by William Kistler, for American Can Company, Neenah, Wisconsin. Grateful thanks to Joseph P. King. Floral Products Manager, for supplying me with the Floratape information.

Repairing or Extending Stems

For certain purposes, stems may be extended or strengthened with wire, picks, and floral tape. Very "juicy" stems may be made stronger by pushing a chenille craft "pipecleaner" wire up the center, then taping on the outside of the stem. Such stems may then be used in floral arrangements or in corsages, without fear that they will break off.

For corsages, all that is needed is wire and tape. For floral designs, a wooden pick is occasionally also utilized.

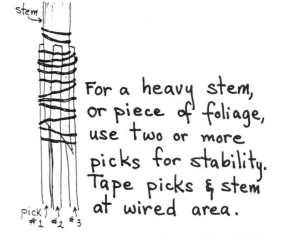

For a heavy stem, or piece of foliage, use two or more picks for stability. Tape picks & stem at wired area.

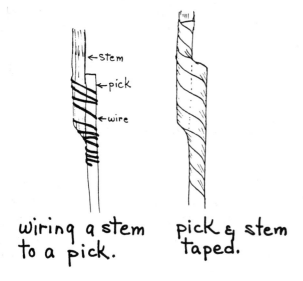

wiring a stem to a pick.

pick & stem taped.

To add a pick to a stem, cut the stem at an angle whenever possible. This is so the wire can be wrapped tightly, spiraling smaller as you go. This will hold it more firmly. Be sure that the pick and stem overlap enough to make a firm stem. If stem is to be inserted into a pin frog, you may have to add some stem at the bottom of the pick, as well. Or plan to push the pick very firmly into florists' clay or attach the pick to some other part of the design. This will prevent the stem from pivoting in the pin frog, which is what it woudl do if you tried to insert the pick itself in the pin frog.

Tape the stem as shown earlier, for corsages. For a show design, wires cannot be seen by the judges, so care should be taken to tape the stem well. Learning how to tape down a stem takes practice to avoid the "chicken-leg" appearance, but is well worth the extra time.

Extending stems for extra length where needed in the design is easily done by placing wire on the stem, as shown. Make sure the wire is strong enough to hold the stem and any foliage without drooping. It would be wise to experiment with non-essential foliage first. Several thin wires can be combined to make a stronger wire. If stem is to go into a design where a pick is needed, add the pick at the bottom of the wire extension. Tape entire stem, down the wire, and over the pick.

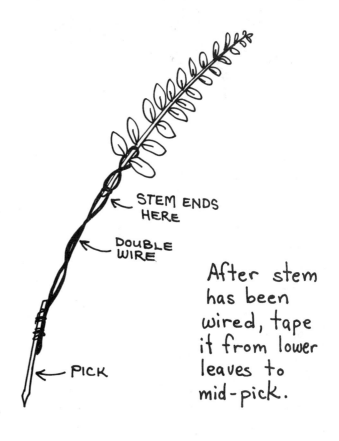

STEM ENDS HERE

DOUBLE WIRE

PICK

After stem has been wired, tape it from lower leaves to mid-pick.

47

An extended stem can be bent in any direction, curved into the desired angle, and add immeasurably to the design if it is done correctly. A little practice with garden foliage will very soon allow you to prepare a design with confidence.

Question – where is the focal point to this floral design?

*AN EXAMPLE OF OVERDOING THE ACCESSORIES: The plant, which **should** be the focal point, is lost!*

When the entire design is in place to your satisfaction, stand back and really evaluate your creation. This is the time to decide if there is a need for further embellishment of a figurine or focal point. At this time experimenting is a must. Use different items of interest, check the colors, size, interest and impact on the overall arrangement. If you are happy with the results, this is fine, but for insurance ask another opinion. This does not have to be another judge or an experienced designer. Some of the most unauthorized opinions may prove to the most beneficial.

Background color and texture play important roles in any design. If the arrangement is to be judged, then the rules of the schedule must be followed. Most clubs have table covers and background material for unity in the overall division, but often a drape or individual background will be allowed. This helps the exhibitor to create color schemes to emphasize and carry out the class theme. Texture of line material is so many times misunderstood in designing with gesneriads, they generally have a graceful growth habit and even the larger leaves have a soft velvety texture. These are so important in planning a design.

Treating Plant Material and Blossoms

These are results of my personal experiments, so I can assure anyone that the only difference in your situation would be the condition of the water being used. I have never used treated, softened, filtered or any type of water other than regular tap water. Most gesneriads will take water through the end of the cut stem. If the stem is cut on an angle, it has more surface to take up water.

Any type of preservative is used to retard algae that forms on the cut part of the stem. If a retardant is not used, the algae will seal the cut

PHOTOGRAPH: RITA DYAN RACTLIFFE

(below)
WEDDING BOUQUET: *An unusual mixture of colors for a memorable event! Red* Aeschynanthus *"Fire Wheel" blossoms, combined with green-edged, pale pink "Shogun" African violets.*

(above)
CORSAGE: *"Watermelon Rose" African violet blossoms highlighted with the* **reddish** **backside** *of* Tricantha Sheidiana *gesneriad leaves.*

PHOTOGRAPH: RITA DYAN RACTLIFFE

ARTISTIC PLANTING: Miniature "Babe" African violet displayed with folded aspidistra leaves, a twisted piece of driftwood and Miorii fern. Little wooden boat was made by John McCoy.

Author Jo McCoy demonstrates her prize-winning design techniques on a STAMOBILE concept seen fully developed in larger photograph.

(below)
STAMOBILE: Weathered root knot becomes a fantasy animal with "neck" of dried seaweed stem, "head" and "plumage" of reddish dried seaweed leaves. The "tail" is pussywillow pips glued to wire. In the body of the STAMOBILE is Aeschynanthus "Fire Wheel", highlighted with the reddish backside of Trican-tha Sheidiana gesneriad leaves, and Spanish moss.

PHOTOGRAPH: RITA DYAN RACTLIFFE

CUT FOLIAGE ARRANGEMENT: A "snake-like" piece of driftwood rises out of an all-foliage design of silvery-velvet *Sinningia Canescens* **leaves. Heavily veined "Smoky Emerald"** *Apicia* **leaves are supported by** *Sinningia Regina* **leaves for background, with drifts of rosemary herb for accent.**

stem, thus preventing water from entering the stem, and causing the turgidity to recede. When this happens the freshness is lost and the need for new material is evident. When material is being treated, if the stem is left longer than needed, a fresh cut about ½" from the end of the stem will allow water to be taken up into the flower to refresh it to normal freshness.

Some of the materials used as retardants to algae are: alcohol, or anything with a high alcohol content, from Listerine to gin. One-fourth teaspoon in a quart of tepid water will not harm delicate flowers or foliage.

NEVER put ice cubes in an arrangement or in treating material. If you used gin to stop the algae, you can add a little tonic and use up the ice cubes more sensibly for drinking, but never put flowers in them.

NEVER use aspirin for anything other than human consumption. (For instance, after drinking too much of the gin and tonic.)

I have been told that a few grains of sugar helps preserve roses, but my experiments have not borne out that theory. However, cutting the stems underwater has proved beneficial in all types of flowers. When cutting any plants or flowers that grow outside, it is best to take a container of tepid water and put the flowers in it as soon as they are cut. Early morning or late afternoon is the best time to cut any outside plants.

Professional florists use a commercial product that is a granular texture and dissolves in water readily. I used it for years in my florist shops. I guess it is a matter of habit, but if the stems are cut daily, and fresh water added, I have found the flowers will last just as long. One reason this product is used so much is a busy shop does not have the time or personnel to give all the flowers daily care.

Corsage making needs a bit different treatment. Stems should be cut shorter, as the wiring of the blossoms create the stem, and makes a neater, less bulky corsage. I use a shallow container, muffin or pie plate. Small pieces of fern are good to keep the flower out of water, but let the stem be submerged in the tepid water. If using natural leaves for the background, they should be treated in the same way.

The most important principle in floral design is the *courage* to put into effect your own concepts and ideas.

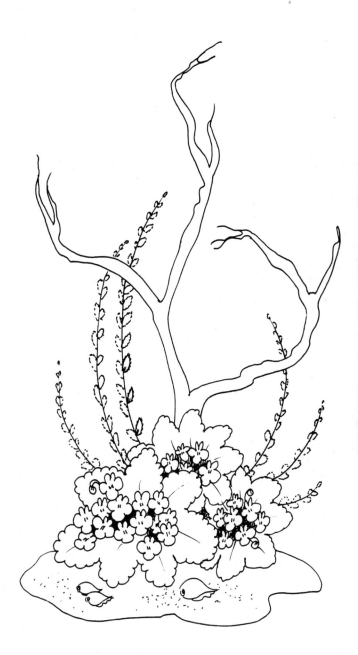

What a difference! Bleach the driftwood, cluster the violets, remove hard-edged fern and replace with pussywillows, soften base with sand, add a few little shells.

Temporary Artistic Planting – with variations

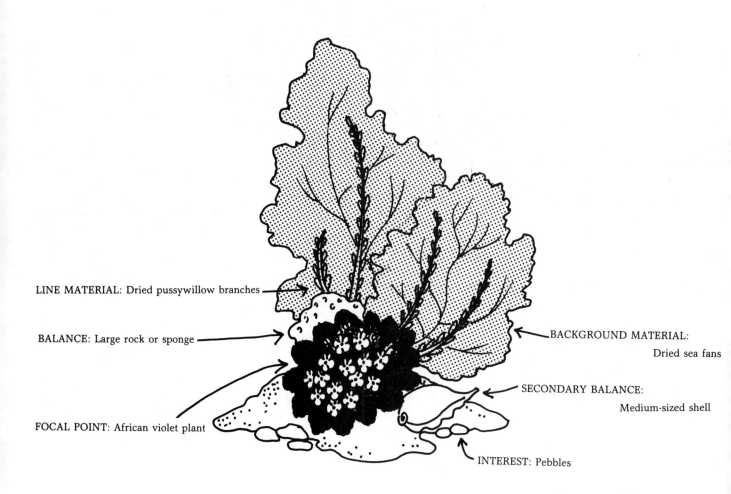

LINE MATERIAL: Dried pussywillow branches

BALANCE: Large rock or sponge

BACKGROUND MATERIAL: Dried sea fans

FOCAL POINT: African violet plant

SECONDARY BALANCE: Medium-sized shell

INTEREST: Pebbles

BASE: Sand over plywood base

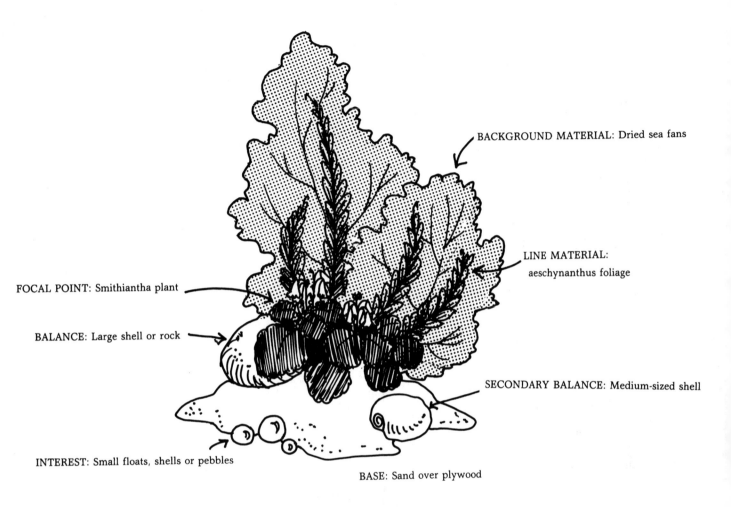

BACKGROUND MATERIAL: Dried sea fans

LINE MATERIAL:
aeschynanthus foliage

FOCAL POINT: Smithiantha plant

BALANCE: Large shell or rock

SECONDARY BALANCE: Medium-sized shell

INTEREST: Small floats, shells or pebbles

BASE: Sand over plywood

The difference between
a *planter* and a *planting*:

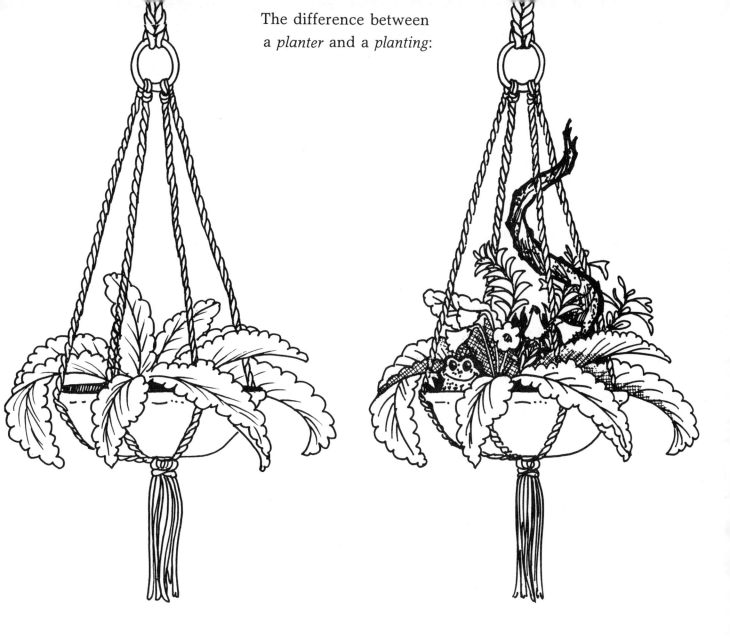

Hanging garden with *streptocarpus*,

Hanging garden with *streptcarpus*,
aeschynanthus, and *sinningia* with
driftwood and frog figurine.

CHAPTER VI

Artistic Plantings (Permanent)

These plantings are considered permanent because they may be kept in the same container for years with an occasional light pruning. They must have a design; the difference is that we must achieve a good arrangement in a controlled area. The small space means we must use miniature,

53

or small, growing plants as well as small rocks, figurines, bits of driftwood, etc. Proportion plays a major part in the design of these plantings.

If you plan to use figurines, it is best to try them well in advance of the time they are to be shown. If they fail to add to the overall design, then omit them and try to bring out the theme of the design in other ways. An old adage in arrangement: when in doubt, leave it out.

One rule that I follow in planting any of these gardens is: place the background plants first, then observe and plan the rest of the design. Generally, the forward plants form the focal point of the planting, so I add these for the final part. It is much easier to change the plants in front than the others. The background plants usually contain the line material, and the general formation of the landscape in the design. The plants in the foreground are easier to reach without disturbing the main structure.

These containers have no drainage provisions, so we must be very careful about overwatering. If using the container for the first time, it is advisable to measure the water. A container with a long spout is a good investment. It is easy to add the water (warm) around the outside edge, or in the case of a terrarium, let the water wash down the glass wall or side. Use less water than you think it will need, let it set overnight, then if necessary add more until the soil is just slightly moist.

Terrariums

When I plant terrariums, I start with a clean, dry container. For a first try at planting terrariums, I would suggest a five gallon fish aquarium. Yard sales are a great source for these. If they do not have a cover, a good substitute is plastic wrap with a few pencil holes in the top. Most aquariums are standard size and new covers with lights may be purchased from the local aquatic supply store or pet shop.

When the container is clean it is best to let it sit overnight in a dry place. This prevents the soil from clinging to the sides as the plants are being arranged.

A dining table is a good place to work, as you

can see each step as the creation is in progress. In a five gallon container I use two cups of charcoal in the bottom, then about two quarts of coarse sponge-rock. The sponge-rock is placed in the center in a mound, so that none of it shows

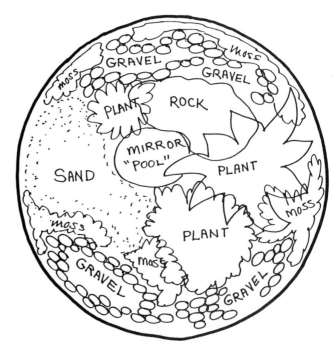

TOP VIEW OF PLANTED CONTAINER

at the edge of the glass. This size container will take four or five quarts of potting soil. I keep the soil very shallow in front and deeper in the back of the container. This is the time to decide the type of landscape you are planning. I sometimes mound the soil in one back corner about two-thirds of the height, place a good-sized piece of volcanic rock on top so it rests against the back, and let the soil gently slope down to the opposite corner. With my hand I push the soil firmly from the rock to a strategic point that will accomodate a simulated pool or fountain. The taller plants should be placed in the background or corner behind the rock. From this point it is the designer's option as to the arrangement and planting. At the spot where the blooming plants are to be placed, I suggest "planting" a pot of the same size as the one the blooming plant is growing in. This will be the focal point and it is easy to fill in the rest of the landscape to fit that particular space.

As you work, keep the "path" firm, then when everything is in place put a small mirror or clear plastic circle just beneath the soil at the lower end of the trail, fill the trail with aquarium gravel to blend with the focal point, or use natural colored gravel. If a waterfall would interest the designer, a four-inch by fifteen-inch strip of plastic wrap, pulled lengthwise until it is stretched, gives the impression of water. Secure it behind the rock and pull it tight over a crevice in the rock into the "pool" at the foot of the rock.

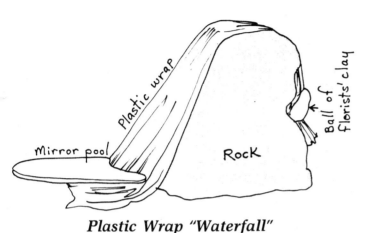

Plastic Wrap "Waterfall"

Plastic wrap pulled under mirror & secured
Ball of florlist's clay to secure plastic wrap or pull wrap under rock to secure

Another way of constructing a waterfall takes a bit more time but it is well worth the effort. Select the rock or driftwood or a combination of several natural-looking combinations. Place them in the position they will be in the terrarium, then melt a light blue candle and gently pour the wax over the waterfall so it will be natural-looking. After it is dry, mix a slightly deeper blue in with

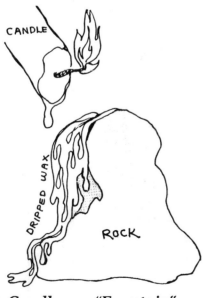

Candlewax "Fountain"

the first color and pour it over the waterfall as a finishing touch. I strongly suggest a practice run at this endeavor for it does take a bit of patience and practice.

When all plants are in place, the remaining soil that is not covered may be planted with any miniature ground cover.

If a minimum of soil is used the plants will not grow as fast, thus requiring less care and pruning.

Water sparingly. Measure the amount of water at the time of planting, use less than you think necessary, and let it set overnight. Then if necessary add small amounts until condensation forms on the inside of the container. If too many droplets form lift the cover and wipe it dry. A terrarium may have moisture on the inside without harming the planting.

If your terrarium is to be entered in a show, be sure to check the schedule. Be sure it follows the theme set forth for that class. I like to plant my terrariums about three months before a show. This gives it the look of an established planting. If I don't know the theme that far in advance, I do the planting in such a way that it can be changed to follow the theme before the show.

Naturalistic Design—Dish Gardens

These gardens and terrariums use a lot of the same basics, for they should depict a scene and carry out the theme chosen for their use.

They are judged for design and arrangement of plantings, suitability of material, condition, color, and distinction. It is important to employ the elements and principles of design and a thorough knowledge of the plant material to be used.

Dish gardens have long been a great source of profit for commercial florists and others engaged in plant lore. These gardens may be most any size or shape. Some are planted in bright colored ceramic containers, animal figures, shells, driftwood and many others. Personally, I prefer the natural wood or terracotta color. Then there is no problem wiht matching, contrasting or blending with a color. There is nothing to detract from the design. The planting procedure is basically the same as a terrarium, the only difference is it is an open container.

Hanging Gardens

A hanging garden may be constructed out of a macrame hanging, with or without a flat or round board in the bottom. Place a dish garden that will fit into that space, on the board, but it is made to hang. You can get ceramic containers, low containers with holes, and use either a decorative cord or an invisible heavy-duty fishing line – nylon monofilament fishing line – to suspend it from a ceiling or wherever you want to hang your garden. A hanging garden can be a terrarium sitting inside the hanger. That is the sort of fun-type thing you can do for your own home, but it is also considered a hanging garden.

Bottle Gardens

I measure the soil I put in, and the water is measured, so once they are in, the bottle garden can be set aside, given as gifts, or whatever.

Because I use miniature African violets for color sometimes and miniature *sinningias*, bottle gardens do need light. Not direct sunlight, because the sun shining through the glass makes it about 105 degrees inside the bottle. I don't think any of our plants would care for that.

Small ferns, miniature ferns, make a nice background for your gesneriads. I use the gesneriads because they take less care and they don't outgrow the bottle or container, or grow out through the top.

Bottle gardens are fun to do, but you don't just drop a bunch of little plants down inside a bottle. You really have to design, and plan a bottle garden. Put your charcoal in the bottom, cover it

"Ralph seems to have a natural knack for bottle gardens!"

"Don't ask silly questions—just hand me the trowel!"

with a mound of sponge rock in the middle, then put in your soil. I use African violet, gesneriad potting mix; I use that same mix for everything I grow.

I use the gallon Almaden tear-shaped wine bottles. They are perfectly round and have a nice shape and make good hanging gardens in a macrame hanger or can be sat on a desk. They make terrific gifts for men, because the way I construct them, they NEVER have to be watered.

These bottle gardens are very interesting, and you can decorate them. I usually take the natural cork that came out of the bottle, and if it is going to   a man, I tie a colored cord on the bottle, and I tie the cork to the neck of the bottle. The cord usually matches or goes with the plants in the bottle. If the bottle goes to a lady, then I use a ribbon to tie the cork on, and often I will make a small corsage of live flowers or ribbon roses. I then attach that to the neck of the bottle, along with the cork.

Those are just ideas. Whatever whimsy strikes you, try it. Who knows? The recipient may like it! These bottles are fantastic to send to hospitals, because they take no care, and the nurses will love you for it.

Another caution pertaining to these is, in a terrarium, it must have a cover and your plant material must not extend above the top of the container. In a dish garden, or an artistic arrangement, your plant material must not extend beyond the boundaries of your designated space. In bottle gardens, this problem is easy to correct,

NO

57

Seedlings

NO   NO

My sister, Jessie Smith, has to my knowledge never even tried to do a design in her life. However, she has a suggestion on what to do with your seedlings. She's entered many, many shows in the horticulture divisions, and has been an AVSA member for many years. She suggests, for shows and displays, PLEASE don't put your unnamed seedlings on the raffle or sales table. Many new members, not knowing the importance of a name on a plant if you are going to enter it in a show, will take home a nameless seedling and grow it up. Then they will wonder why the Entry Committee won't let them enter this lovely plant!

because when the plant starts growing beyond the top, you can just snip it off. You can do that in such a way by carefully cutting the stem just above a leaf note from the back of the plant.

The difference between a seedling and a named variety is that the seedling is just that, a seedling. A named variety must be propagated

"Let's review those basic principles of bubble bowl planting, shall we?"

Clustering seedlings on a hand-built rock. "Glue" pots to rock with floral clay—put spagnum moss between pots to hide mechanics.

———————◆———————

through three generations to prove it will bloom and grow true to the parent plant.

This is not a put-down to seedlings, for they are the life blood of our organizations. Millions of hours of research have been spent to improve on existing cultivars and greater knowledge of new crosses.

Let these seedlings grow, bring them into bloom, and use them in your artistic plantings, in dish gardens, terrariums, and things of that sort. Because in these plantings, the plant itself does not have to have a name, unless the show schedule so states. Entries in the horticulture division must be named varieties and sometimes registered.

Again, your schedule may state that the design must have a named variety, or that the plants must be named varieties. But if the rules do not state this, seedlings are a great source of material for clustering, for greater color. If you want the same color, use several of the same seedlings for clustering. It gives quite an impact.

And seedlings are beautiful; sure, sometimes they are like kittens or sometimes our kids—we think they're beautiful, but everybody doesn't.

Remember, a lot of people don't have much space to grow these seedlings, and they are a little upset when they have worked so hard to bring into bloom a plant that is only a seedling and has no name.

Most shows have a class just for seedlings, but generally they are not entered in any other horticultural classes.

The purpose of entering a show is to create something beautiful, or display something grown and groomed to make it beautiful. In each instance, create and enjoy the fact that the public will enjoy seeing the results of your endeavor.

It is amazing how many 'experienced designers' have entered many times before winning blue ribbons. When I look back at m own record it is hilarious to remember some of the blunders I have made, which proves if we 'hang in there' we may get luck eventually.

Chirita lavandalacea
© 1984 ~ Bjo

"I can't figure out if she's an ordinary nut or one of those flower arrangers!"

CHAPTER VII

Drying and Treating Blossoms and Foliage

The techniques in drying and preserving materials are very interesting. Gathering these materials can be quite an adventure. Among the techniques is drying—air drying, silica gel, borax and cornmeal, or pure white sand—and with glycerine, or with pressing, or skeletonizing. These are the most commonly used ways of treating plant material.

Air Drying

In air drying, you gather the foliage. Now I must say here, I haven't found any of the gesneriad foliage that will air dry successfully. This may not be a fact, but I haven't found any; the silica gel works nicely on such foliage. But back to air drying; this is for line material, filler material, and anything of that sort can be air dried.

Silica Gel & Related Drying Materials

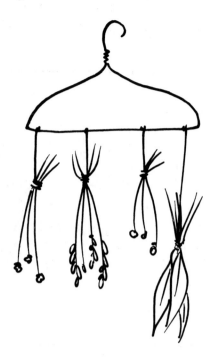

Silica Gel is a granular material used by many professional florists, and it's easy to use. There is also the combination of one-half borax and one-half *white* cornmeal – do not use the yellow – mixed very well. After the mixture is well mixed, sift it so you can be very sure all the lumps are out. Or use white sand, but be sure it is completely dry. When you think it is thoroughly dry, put it in a shallow pan, in a 200 degree oven for at least an hour. Then let it sit in the open air, stirring frequently to make sure you have all the moisture out.

The purpose of the drying material, whether gel, sand, or the borax-cornmeal, is to take all the moisture out of the blossoms and foliage, and dry them. With any of these three methods, I use a large plastic square food container (Tupperware) and put an inch of the drying material in the bottom. Then very carefully lay the blossoms – never mix blossoms and foliage – on the drying material. (Most foliage, branches and leaves are heavier in texture and retain moisture longer, so the chance of crushing delicate blossoms in placing or removing them from the mixture is not worth the risk.) Next I take a small plastic measuring cup with a spout and very carefully pour the drying material over it. If the blossom is tubular flower like a *sinningia* or *aeschynanthus*,

And then if it's not the color you want, spray it with floral spray. This floral spray can be bought at any floral supply shop; it's in a pressure can and comes in about every color imaginable. So this is a very good thing for your line and background material.

Air drying is very simple. I use coat hangers, attaching the lower part of the stem with a string or rubber band to the wire coat hanger. To hang two or three bunches at one time, make a crimp or bend in the hanger to prevent them from sliding together, which would prevent thorough drying from all sides. Then, just hang them in a dry place. A garage is nice, or above a water heater, if it isn't sitting in your kitchen. I gather foliage and flowers, tie them in small bunches, and hang them from the wire coat hangers, until they are fairly dry. Then they can be safely put in boxes or other containers where they will be safe.

Now be careful when treating any of these plants, that they are free of insects. One tiny little ant can demolish a couple of days' work of collecting and drying material. So be sure they are pest-free.

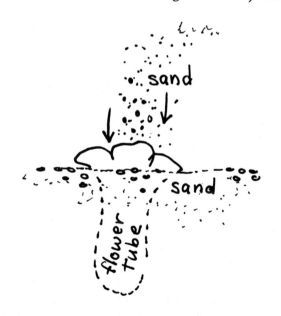

Filling a tubular flower

or any of those, I lay the flower on its back and fill the open end of the flower with the drying material. This way, the tube of the flower does not collapse, and it will dry just as naturally as it is placed. I carefully pour the drying material around the flower, until it completely covers the blossom. I usually start at one end of the box, and go completely over it. I never lay flowers on top of each other.

When the blossoms are thoroughly dry they are very fragile and must be handled very carefully. The drying material should be gently poured from one end onto a newspaper or table top. A pair of tweezers is handy at this point. When the flowers are uncovered to the point, the stem may be picked up with the tweezers, and held upright to brush the surplus gel or sand from the blossom. If a part of the stem is left intact for the drying process, it will be easier to handle in storing.

With African violets, I find that the double blossoms dry beautifully if you lay them flat and pour the drying material very carefully into and around all the petals. All of the other flowers I have used – *aeschynanthus, sinningia cardinalis*, any long or tubular flowers – be sure the tube is full of drying material. Your flowers should be as natural-looking as possible, for this is the way they will dry.

The container, by the way, should be about four inches deep; it must be deep enough to place a full inch of drying material over the top of the flowers. It's very interesting, by the way; I have found not many gesneriad blossoms change color or fade in silica gel, which is the only thing I have tested so far. African violets, or at least some varieties, will change color and fade slightly. White African violets will turn cream color, and not be stark white. Blues, and especially dark blues, will turn darker. I find that if you make a powder of just ordinary blackboard chalk – you can get it in all colors – and push it through a screen, or sift it, to make a powder. Then put it in a plastic bag, drop your blossoms in it, one at a time, and gently shake the bag. This will "pouf" the blossoms with the colored chalk powder, and they will dry with that color on them. This is especially effective with dark blue violets.

This can be done with any color of blossoms, pink and so on. I did not find that treating white blossoms helped in any way. An interesting thing: a white blossom with a green edge is very pretty because it comes out cream color with a green edge. So don't be shy about using your white blossoms, because they are very beautiful.

"Oh, Knock it off! I didn't use **all** your chalk!"

Skeletonizing Foliage

You can treat heavily-textured leaves by skeletonizing them. Of course, your color, form, and sometimes texture are altered by this process of preserving. The leaves to be skeletonized should be removed from the branches and placed in a solution of one tablespoon sal soda to each quart of water. Boil this for 30 to 60 minutes with the leaves in it, then allow to cool, without removing the leaves. Try not to crowd the leaves, or you might distort them. Then place the leaves on a sinkboard or any flat surface, and scrape away the fleshy part of each leaf with a nylon or other kind of brush with firm bristles. Brush until all the pulp or fleshy parts are off the leaf and the skeleton or veins are all that is left.

Place the skeleton leaves in a solution of 2 tablespoons bleach to 1 quart of water for just about an hour. Any kind of bleach will do. Then remove the bleached leaves, and rinse them in cold water. These skeleton leaves will be cream color. Dry them between sheets of absorbent paper, then press them under weights just as you dried and pressed under newspaper. If you want colored skeleton leaves, they can be sprayed with floral spray or any number of other paints. I personally think they are beautiful just as they come out of the bleach, because the cream color is very conducive to attractive floral arrangements.

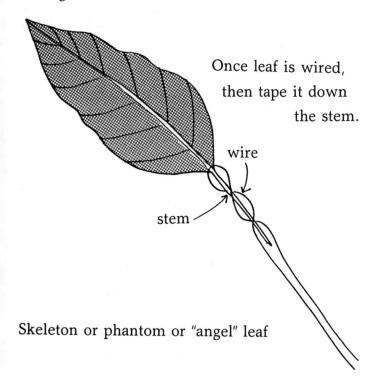

Once leaf is wired,

then tape it down

the stem.

wire

stem

Skeleton or phantom or "angel" leaf

Skeletonized leaves are available for sale under brand names such as "Angel Feathers." It is probably easier to purchase such leaves, rather than take the time and effort to make skeleton or phantom leaves yourself. Such leaves should be wired and taped, just like a green leaf.

Skeleton leaves may be sprayed with florists' spray to obtain any color desired. They may also be pressed with a warm iron to shape the leaf as needed. These leaves may also be rolled up wet and allowed to dry, for yet another effect. Skeleton leaves make a pretty net-like background that does not interfere with your design, but still fills it in

nicely. They are especially good used with smaller African violet plants that might otherwise be overpowered by larger background foliage.

Phantom Leaves

Phantom or skeleton leaves are the ghostly remnants of the leaves that have waved on the trees in summer. They are troublesome to prepare, but are very pretty when finished. Gather the leaves when they are perfect, and then lay them in a large jar, filled with water. Leave them there until they decay, when the fleshy part of the leaves can be easily detached from the framework.

The translucent, thread-like form of this delicate veined work is very beautiful. Having loosened the green part, bleach the remainder by infusion in a strong solution of soda.[1] When quite white, bouquets or wreaths may be made of different leaves in combination, which may be arranged on a dark background, or set under glass.

from **The Fireside Library of Useful Knowledge**
edited by Charles Morris (W.E. Scull, 1902)

[1]The "soda" mentioned is sal soda, or a caustic bleaching soda.

Skeleton Leaves, To Make

Steep the leaves, seed-vessels, or other parts of the plant to be dissected, in rain water, until the whole of the soft matter is decomposed. Some require a few weeks others several months. The rotted parts are now to be carefully removed with a fine brush, under the surface of water, or in a stream of water. A syringe is sometimes required.

To bleach the skeletons soak them from some hours in a mixture of 1 oz. of strong solution of chloride of lime[2] and a quart of distilled water.

Lastly, wash thoroughly in cold water, and dry by exposure to air.

from **The Druggist's General Receipt Book**
by Henry Beasley (Lindsay & Blakiston, 1872)

[2]Chloride of lime, a strong disinfectant bleach, was used in solutions of 1 ounce of 200 gallons of water for normal use; in the solution suggested here, it would be very strong indeed! Chlorine bleach will accomplish the same results.

Pressing Foliage & Flowers

In preserving and siliconizing, your foliage can be pressed in several thicknesses of newspaper. Do not use the colored pages or slick, shiny paper. Don't overlap the leaves, or they will stick together. Use several thicknesses of newspaper and cover the leaves with several thicknesses more. Then you can place more foliage on top of that, and you can treat several layers of foliage

*"Doggone it, Jo! This is carrying
   pressing your @*‡¶®! plants too far!"*

this way. When this is done, place the stack of newspapers on a flat, hard surface. Then cover this with a piece of plywood and heavy weights on top. Use heavy rocks or something like that; I find that a couple of gallon jugs, filled with water, are very good. Or use bags filled with sand or gravel. Use anything that will hold the stack firm and in place. Put the whole pile in a warm, dry place. It will take 3 to 4 weeks before the drying process is completed. Sometimes if the foliage is very moist, you'll need to change the newspapers and replace them with dry newspaper. Then press the foliage again until it is really stiff and dry.

Glycerine Preserving

Some of the foliage that may be preserved in glycerine are the aspidistra — here in California, they grow in the yard — and American beech, eucalyptus, myrtle, crabapple, English ivy, magnolia, Oregon grape, purple-leaf plum, poplar — either silver or white — flowering quince, salal, oak, *ti* plant, and many other foliages. If you see something you think would be very pretty, experiment!

Some of our most original conceptions of design have evolved from curiosity and experimentation.

Treating Foliage

Treating branches and foliage often brings about a very nice change in color. Particularly the silver-dollar or "baby" eucalyptus, magnolia leaves, oak leaves, ivy, and many other beautiful foliages which can be treated with glycerine. Magnolia leaves, in particular, have a beautiful velvety texture on the back side.

The glycerine solution is one part commercial glycerine to two parts hot water. If using reasonably short branches or oak leaves, and individual leaves, I like to put them in a glass container. This is because the solution should be three to four inches deep, and in glass, you can tell when the level is down and should be replenished. When the level drops, don't add more glycerine, just add more warm water back to the original level.

It takes from five to six weeks for branches and leaves to become soft and flexible. The glycerine causes these branches to become very pliable. it is a joy to work with them, and of course, they can be used many, many times. If kept properly, they can be kept from one year to the next, packed loosely in cardboard cartons.

With taller, longer branches, I crush the stems with a hammer on a flat surface, and put them in hot water. Be sure that the longer branches are in water at least four inches deep. These tall branches don't have to be in a glass container; I use an old granite canning vessel. But you do have to be careful about the water level. In a larger container, the longer branches stand upright and the shape stays much better.

This is the time, when you put them in the water, to put a little curve to a branch, if it doesn't have a natural curve. Select a lead fishing weight that has a loop on the end of it, and attach that near the end of the branch, to bend it in the position that you want to use it. Let it be treated in that way, as it stands in the glycerine, and the branch will hold that position when you take it out of the water.

"Hey, hon—have the danged kids been in my fishing gear again?"

Line Material

Care and Treatment; Preserving

Line and background material may be fresh, dried or "treated." There is no rule that a special rock or piece of driftwood must be one piece or the shape it was when originally found. Be inventive – it is very interesting to see the different forms a certain piece of wood will take by turning it in different directions, taking one or the other end, or center. Try leaving the smooth hard wood, and carving out all soft or decayed parts, then reassembling in an interesting form to highlight a design. A chisel or dull knife are good tools.

BLEACHING: to bleach or change color of any wood takes time but the overall effect is well worth the effort. After all the soft wood has been removed, wash the piece of wood in warm water, then submerge it in a solution of one cup household bleach to three gallons of warm water. Leave it overnight (if the wood floats, it must be weighted down to keep all parts underwater). After the soaking period, it should be removed from the solution and dried in the hot sun, turning it frequently to bleach on all sides. If you wish a very light color, the procedure may be repeated two or three times. Rinse in clear water before using in an arrangement.

NEUTRALIZING: objects from the beach or ocean that have been in salt water. Sea shells, rocks, driftwood or weathered wood must be treated before using in any design with fresh material. Soak the item in a solution of one cup household ammonia to three gallons of warm water. All items must be totally submerged in the solution overnight, then removed and rinsed several times in clear water, and sun-dried.

The reason for these procedures – salt water will cause burns on fresh plants. Untreated wood will cause mold, mildew or growth of strange looking mushrooms and fungi.

*Bĵo Trimble sketching one of her mother's **aeschynanthus purposii variegated**.*

CHAPTER VIII

On the Trail of Design Material (Likely Locations)

On the Trail of Design Material (Likely Locations)

Locating design material can become a fascinating hobby, as well as creating many friendships.

For starters, listen to comments at flower shows like: "I have a lovely Cypress knee that I brought from a trip to the South. I would like to see it used in an arrangement." "I have some nice pink quartz from a rock shop in South Dakota." Your comment might be to the effect that if they brought the item to a meeting, you're sure someone would be able to suggest something to bring out the beauty in using it with gesneriads for everyone's enjoyment. Shows are the greatest source of design material, especially if you don't have time for a lot of travel.

Gem and mineral shows can produce a great challenge for original designs. Our friends who are members of the local Gem and Mineral Society tell me that pieces of 'rocks' may be 'tumbled', then removed before they are fully polished, for dull or matte finish, still retaining all their color. All rock-hounds have a wealth of design material somewhere in their backyard. Most of them were gathered with the thought they might be valuable, but when cut turned out be genuine "Leaverite" (as in "leave 'er right there") or "Bird Rocks" (their only use it to throw at birds). Nevertheless these are the ones *we* can use to great advantage. Don't hesitate to build or construct your own rock by using two or more for the desired height or width and design. The thing to watch here is use the same color or shade of rock. Clever incorporation of weathered wood is effective.

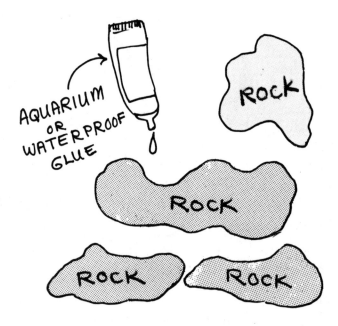

Build one large rock with several small ones. Use chisel & hammer or other tools to chip or carve rock to fit together as needed.

Some 'Rock-Hounds' have their own tumblers and rock cutting equipment that is used to get the pattern or grain of the inside of a large rock. These are cut in slabs about three-eighths to one-fourth inch thick. Before they are polished, they have a lovely soft finish, and most have colors in light pastels. These make very effective bases and backgrounds for miniature arrangements. At shows these are sometimes sold in boxes of three or five. These are not 'gem quality', but that is not our purpose at this time.

Mini-Sinningia displayed on a Brazilian agate slab with another slab as back ground.

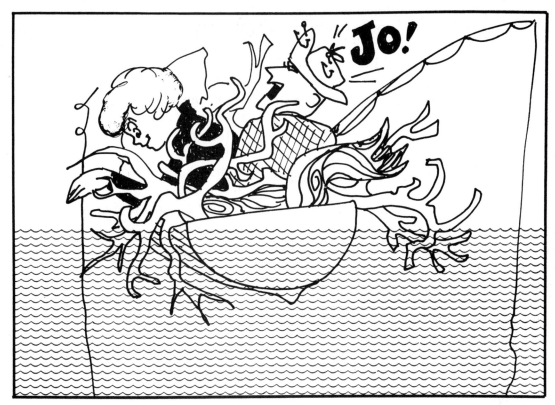

A word of caution here: when rocks are "slabbed" (sliced or cut by rockhounds for polishing), a very heavy machine oil is used on the rock saw. Before using with any plant material, wash all rocks thoroughly with a detergent.

The 'barter' system works well in collecting. John and I do a lot of fishing, but don't care to eat our catch. Our 'Rock-Hound' friends enjoy our catch and bring us weathered wood, manzanita and rocks. This adds up to a great get-together and a lot of kidding from husbands.

PLACES TO LOOK FOR ROCKS: Some semi-precious or "gemmy" rocks can be found on beaches, in riverbeds, and in the desert or

mountain areas of most states; any rock or lapidary shop will have a "rockhounding in XX area" booklet for sale that will tell you where to find your own rocks and interesting mineral specimens. An easier method is to find rockhounds at the gem and mineral exhibits in county fairs, at swap meets, gem and mineral shows, rock shops and even garage sales. Talk to people, tell them what you need and offer to trade for plants or a terrarium. All rockhounds love to barter and trade; they all have rocks they cannot use, for one reason or another, as either a "cutting" rock or a good "cabinet specimen" to just show off. This is the piece of rock they'll be glad to give away, just to see it get a good home, because that rock cost them some time and effort. Sometimes you can also *borrow* a really fine crystal specimen or unusual slab of rock, just for one show, if you promise to take good care of it.

WARNING: Some minerals, such as sulphur crystals, are exceptionally beautiful but will crumble or powder, contaminating your plant. Many seemingly stable minerals are hygroscopic (absorbing water from the air) and will disintegrate during the show; be sure to ask the rockhound about this.

Fishing trips are great for exercise, fresh air, collecting rocks, driftwood, cones, pods, grasses and sometimes catching fish. They can also be

71

hazardous to your health (like Spouse tossing you overboard, or warning "one more stick in this boat and we sink"). When we go fishing and I don't catch fish, I gather driftwood, etc. I wouldn't say I am a lousy fisherman, but our backyard is half full of driftwood.

Nurseries are a good source of all kinds of line, background and filler material. We have traded with the same nursery since we have been in Bakersfield. I suppose they consider us a good customer or at any rate they allow me to 'prune' most any of the larger shrubs and trees. I never misuse this privilege, but usually I need only one or two branches, and it does not detract from the attractiveness of the shrub or tree. Most eucalyptus need constant pruning and many others can benefit from a neat trim occasionally. So be a friend to your local nurseryman. It pays good dividends in cuttings.

Beachcombing is another rich source of line and accent material. The important thing to remember here is to wash materials thoroughly, then treat as explained in Chapter VII. Pencil-sized driftwood is ideal for cross-bars when assembling a mobile. It is very lightweight and easy to drill small holes for the fishline. Sometimes interesting shells are passed up because they are broken, but when designing a beach scene the shells are not always on top of the sand. Push the broken edge of the shell into the sand or cover the broken part with fern or other greenery. Use two shells interlocked, with the broken portion away from the front of the design. If an object looks interesting to you, it is sure to interest the viewers.

Nature walks on woodland trails, beaches and auto travel are good prospects for the unusual and much sought after design material. In traveling we see many roadside businesses that have native wood, rock, Cypress knees, manzanita branches, pussy willow, cork oak and many items not available in our own locality. Just keep on the lookout and don't believe your spouse when he says he can't find a place to get off the road.

Accessories

Miniature supply houses are an excellent source for figurines, small animal and bird figures. They are usually made to scale of one inch to one foot (1/12), and this helps take care of proportion. Care should be taken to compare these figures with the overall size of the design. When given a choice, it is better to use one too small than one too large. Two small animals will bring out a theme more sharply than one oversized. You are painting a picture with the designs.

A word of caution here: try the design and leave it in a spot where you may observe it over a period of several days, adding and removing objects until a satisfactory combination is reached.

Of course, you have to take into consideration your schedule. Be sure you consult your schedule to find out the space you are allowed. Sometimes in the terrarium class, you don't have a space requirement, but in all other designs, you do. Check your schedule; I have neglected it myself, and I know others who have laughingly said, later, that it would have been a good idea if they *had* read the schedule. You can't know your show schedule too well, if you want to go for that blue ribbon. And all you have to do is goof on that one little detail and you've lost your ribbon.

Violet design with blue-and-white ceramic Dutch mill, natural pussywillows & floral sprayed blue silver-dollar eucalyptus. Note most of base is covered with a cloth drape.

COLUMNEA "YELLOW DRAGON"

74

DESIGN: *1. to plan and delineate . . .8. the arrangement of parts, details, form, color, etc., especially so as to provide a complete and artistic unit. [Webster's 20th Century Dictionary]*
1. a plan or scheme conceived in the mind and intended for subsequent execution; the preliminary conception of an idea that is to be carried into effect by action; a project.
[The Oxford English Dictionary]

CHAPTER IX

The Principles and Elements of Design

The design is different from a bouquet in that a design is the act of composing; arrangement of elements[1] in artistic form. The fundamental principles of design should govern all our works of art. A bouquet is a more impromptu creation. With practice, some arrangements are easy to translate into form and shape for a design. In working with a specific theme, it sometimes takes some extra thought and planning.

The Oxford English Dictionary[1] accepts *"principle"* and *"element"* as fundamentally having the same meaning. Traditional use of these terms in the gesneriad world has been, so far, to divide basic design components under either one of the two terms. Since a good design should take *all* the

---

[1]*PRINCIPIUM: (Latin: Principia) Beginning,* **origin, source,** *foundation,* **ELEMENT** *[Oxford English Dictionary]*

PRINCIPLE: *1. ultimate* **source, origin** *or cause of something,*
3. fundamental truth [Webster's 20th Century Dictionary]
I. **origin, source** *of action,*
II. fundamental truth, law or motive force,
III. rudiment, **ELEMENT,** *essence,*

components into consideration, it probably doesn't matter if you recognize them as *"principles"* or *"elements"* in the long run. However, if you plan to take the test to become an African violet or gesneriad judge, all should be memorized exactly as stated below:

The Principles of Design are *balance, contrast, dominance, rhythm, proportion*, and *scale*. The fundamental principles of design should govern all of our works of art.

There are two kinds of balance: symmetrical and asymmetrical. Symmetrical balance is the equal balancing of weight and involves the actual matching of flower for flower in form and size on each side of the container, or leaf for leaf in a visual balance.

Asymmetrical balance is acquired by using more weight on one side than the other. A carefully selected accessory may be used to achieve the balance necessary. Stability of materials is a judging point in show entries. There must be a satisfying relationship between the parts, such as: the center of interest should be low and near the vertical axis. The lighter colors and smaller flowers should be toward the top and outer edges of the design. Darker colors should be kept low in the design. If small flowers are to be used for the focal point, they should be clustered together for greater impact in the center of interest. Keep a feeling of openness at the outer parts of the arrangement.

Contrast is to show differences, diversity of adjacent parts in color, emotion, tone or brightness. To achieve this will add interest by contrast of texture and line material, or subtle use of blending tones.

Dominance dictates that one line or form must dominate to avoid monotony. Texture and color will aid in giving unity to the design.

If different shapes of flowers are to be used in the arrangement they must not be used in equal amounts. One must dominate the other, also this is true in using colors. Repeat the flower color in some other material to emphasize the dominant tone.

Rhythm is suggested movement. This carries the eye through the design smoothly, not allowing it to become distracted, or move from one part to another. Rhythm may be accomplished by several different methods: line repetition, intensity of color properly placed and accessories in proper proportion. Rhythm provides the organizing principle, a logical path to carry the eye easily through and around the design. It may be created by line, direction, repetition, transition or graduation.

I have heard it said that one should leave strategic spaces "for the butterflies to get through."

10a. *earliest or* **elementary** *parts of a subject of study;* **ELEMENTS** *or rudiments,*
11. *a component part, ingredient, constituent,* **ELEMENT** *. . .source. . .originate[Oxford English Dictionary]*
ELEMENT: *A first* **PRINCIPLE**, 3. *a natural or fitting environment for a person or thing. [Webster's 20th Century Dictionary]*
I. *a component part of a complex whole,*
III. 13. *primordial* **PRINCIPLE**, **source** *or* **origin**
IV. 14. *. . .also the first* **PRINCIPLES** *of an art or science [The Oxford English Dictionary]*

*"Well, that **does** integrate the design with the figurine...sorta..."*

When planning a design, sometimes the odd things we try work out very well, and everyone likes it, but we are not particularly impressed. Some of the designs we work at for hours just seem to lack that certain touch.

If you like doing designs, don't wait to enter a show or have a special occasion for an excuse. I won't say "practice makes perfect," for in thirty years I haven't achieved that goal; but I will admit that practice gives me more confidence. I sometimes do several different designs for one theme, then choose the one I like best when the time comes to enter a show, and hope the judges think so as well.

Proportion and scale are very closely related. They deal with the relationship between plant material, container, accessories, and placement of the design.

The completed arrangement should have a visual appearance of proper proportion. This includes the container, and it should be large enough to support the plant material and still give a feeling of a complete picture. The entire picture should have a good proportion and correct scale. When using figurines or any type of accessory, scale is of the utmost importance. Suitability of materials is a judging point not to be ignored. Large figurines are the most common fault in designs and they tend to detract from the entire arrangement. If we must use a large figurine to carry out a theme, then I would suggest using it in the background of the design, with foliage or plant material obscuring at least the lower part. In this way it has the appearance of being smaller and less conspicuous, but still support the theme of the arrangement.

The number two offender dealing with accessories is using too much, or too many. Instead of a whole family of cute squirrels scampering over a rock or a piece of driftwood, probably one or two would create the same impression. Most all animals show movement to bring rhythm to a design, but too many or too big can detract from proportion and scale.

Self-esteem goes hand in hand with creativity. Anyone can do designs if they make up their minds to do so, and most important of all, work at it.

Experimentation is of the utmost importance when working with gesneriads. Some will last longer than others as cut material. African violets are generally very fragile, but some varieties hold up very well in corsages and arrangements. However, the ones that look as if they would last longer, sometimes do not hold the turgidity long enough to be used in these designs. The safest procedure is to find a variety the color to be used, and experiment. These results should be kept in a record book for reference at any time.

My introduction to the other gesneriads was using the leaves and foliage as line and background material. They are easy to wire and curve into any line necessary. The colors, texture and adaptability have endeared them to me for years. Properly pre-conditioned, they will keep fresh for many days after a show. My Scotch ancestry would not permit me to discard anything still usable, so I planted the cuttings. One day some *aeschynanthus* 'Black Pagoda' bloomed for me, and that did it, I was "hooked".

Some of the plants that I have used, both blossoms and foliage, that last well in arrangements are *Streptocarpus, Aeschynanthus, Nematanthus, Sinningia, Smithianthia* and many more. Try some of these arrangements with the back side of the leaves showing from the front of the design. Some of the textures and colors are really beautiful.

Elements of Design

The elements of design are the working ingredients of the tangible concepts of: *space, color, line, form, size, texture* and *pattern*. An intangible concept is *character*.

LINE is the primary foundation of the design. It is a visual path, and due to its direction and character, it arouses certain emotional responses in the observer. Line may be severe and masculine, exhibiting strength and vitality, or it may be feminine and whimsical, suggesting gentleness and delicacy. Line gives a feeling of growth and life in a design. The Line should not be broken; if it is, it gives a feeling of nervousness and confusion.

Line is achieved by the shape and the forms of the design. It may be manifested by actual Line material, or repetition of shapes and colors.

SPACE, for a design, is very important. It depends on where the design will be placed; if your space is restricted as in a show, you must remember to always take measurements of the area. Remember: measure twice and design once. It helps to measure and take down all the measurements. Your space is an imaginary frame to separate your design from other displays, or to separate it from other furniture or other items in your home. Your space influences the size, shape and direction of the design. Space is achieved by visualizing that you are working on a picture with a frame. It may be bounded by actual lines, as of a niche, or imaginary, such as set by a piece of furniture or a pedestal. It would be planned in relation to this frame. Your placement of lines determines space.

FORM: Many designs are based on geometric forms or combinations of forms, such as the sphere, the cube, the pyramid, or the pyramid triangle. The triangle is the simplest form for general purposes.

Establish line of height, which should be the length plus the width of the container. Two types of flowers, elongated or spike, and round structures. A framework. Results in form closely related to line.

PATTERN is a silhouette of your design; solids and voids, variety in size and form, to create a pattern in any design.

TEXTURE modifies color and weight of a composition. Shiny material appears lighter and brighter. Coarse, dull material appears darker and heavier.

COLOR has emotional impact and plays a strong role in determining the mood of a design. There should be harmony of color. Knowledge of color relationship is very valuable in creating flower arrangements. An arrangement may have very good design, but lack good use of color. Too many colors are distracting and cluttered. Whatever colors are used must be skillfully proportioned and blended. A judge must then be very careful not to permit personal color preferences to interfere with a fair evaluation.

CHARACTER is the degree of refinement or elegance of the material. Texture may be contrasted successfully, but not character.

DISTINCTION has to do with the materials and techniques.

ORIGINALITY has to do with self-expression. Your designs must emanate your own personality. Don't try to copy someone else. In the first, this is not original; in the second place, you may find copying works out poorly.

INSPIRATION: to do a successful design, your inspiration comes from the development of a

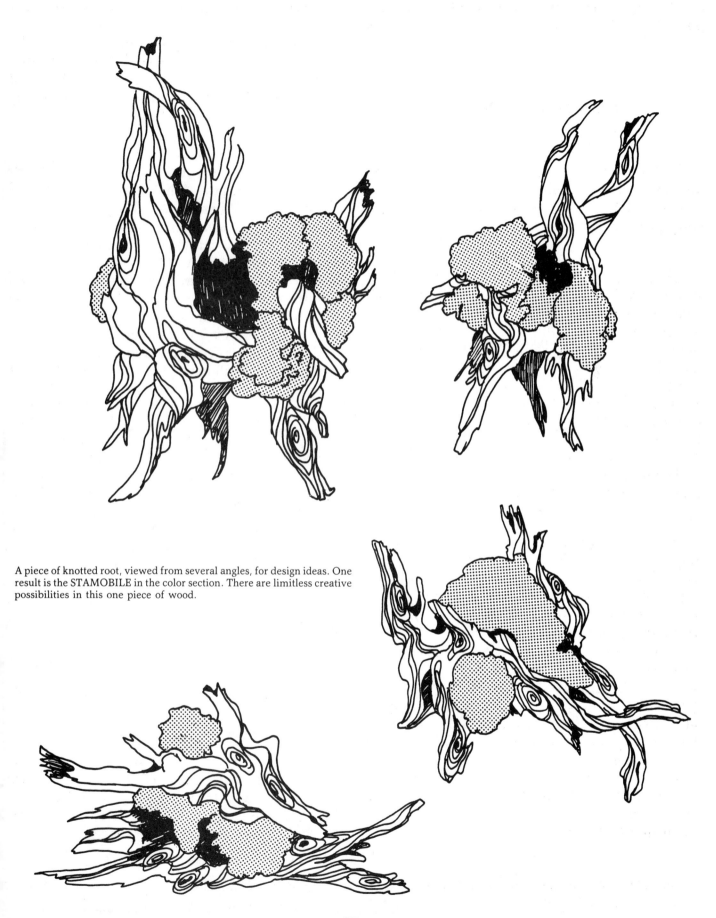

A piece of knotted root, viewed from several angles, for design ideas. One result is the STAMOBILE in the color section. There are limitless creative possibilities in this one piece of wood.

"seeing eye." Always be on the lookout for unusual foliage and a way of using them. You don't always have to use foliage face forward or the way it grows naturally. The back side of many gesneriad cultivars are more interesting from the back, from a designer's point of view, than they are from the front.

Always visualize how these things will look, with possibly the blossoms from another gesneriad than their own flowers. Many of the gesneriads have beautiful foliage and other insignificant flowers. Don't ever hesitate to mix them, but keep in mind the blending of the colors.

WORKSPACE: Your best workshop is right in your own home. A table, where you can try a design and leave it sitting so you can look at it, is necessary. And you'll be surprised at how, over a period of two or three days, how many things you will find to change on a design.

I'd like to quote a paragraph from the *AVSA Judge's and Exhibitors Handbook*: "Inspiration: you may acquire this from books, your home, friends and nature. Aspiration: you must be willing to try. You can look at designs all day and say 'Oh, that looks so easy,' but you must be willing to try, yourself. Motivation: you must be willing to work at it; don't expect me to do a blue-ribbon design the very first try. Believe me, designers who walk away with blue ribbons in shows could probably tell you a lot of funny incidents. But you must be willing to work at it. Education: you must have an open mind. When you see designs or when you see a book on designs, regardless of what the book is designing, you can take a design meant for an iris and modify it to suit your own taste as far as gesneriads. Imagination: originality is the yardstick of an open mind with vision. You can visualize; you get an idea, or see unusual plant material, or ordinary plant material in an unusual design. We must keep in mind that different areas in the country will have plants we would consider

"A workspace where I can leave the design sitting? Surely she jests!!"

Conditioning cut flowers & foliage in a muffin tin

rare or unusual, but to local residents they would seem common. Communication: we must be able to project or communicate our ideas to other people. The judges must be able to interpret your ideas to properly judge the entry. Next in importance is the enjoyment the general public will derive from the entry. When we do a design and are pleased with the results, that is not enough – the judges must be able to interpret the obvious concept of the design. All judges will try very hard to accept the communicating factors."

Most shows have classes for arrangements, and this means that all materials must be cut flowers and foliage. No plants or any growing material may be used in these classes. Home or office decorations are for personal pleasure, and you may do as you wish. All cut material should be conditioned or 'hardened off' prior to beginning the arrangement. When line or background material has a firm texture it should be washed, even if it looks clean. Dust particles could lose the entry some points on condition, therefore cleanliness is a must in all show entries. Cleaning and conditioning may be done at the same time, as submerging in water is generally sufficient to 'harden off' most plant material. In some instances using this method and leaving them in water overnight is suitable. The best advice I can give you is: experiment well in advance of the time you wish to use the material.

The theme of the show sets the mood and the space allowed is of prime importance. Choose the container, select and condition all plant material, take time to evaluate each step in the design. If the colors and textures blend well, and all else is in harmony, then create and enjoy for the true pleasure of creating a thing of beauty.

Basic Design Elements

The basic elements of any floral design are: a focal point, a primary line or the line material, a base line. Secondary elements are: balance, any secondary or intermediate lines, background. Tertiary elements are the interest and filler. Using these basics, any variety of creative designs may be achieved by applying yourself to practice and more practice. Very few people can "throw something together" without lots of knowledge, experience and practice. The next time you envy someone their ability to "effortlessly" create a design, remember the extra, unseen work that went into that apparent ease.

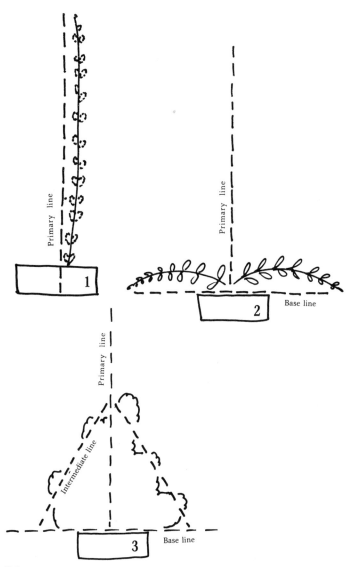

Keep in mind that there is no rigid rule about keeping the design within a prescribed "oval" or "triangle". These terms mercly describe the design style, not the exact shape of the arrangement. Bits of the design may extend beyond the shape described below and still fit in that design style. Foliage may be judiciously trimmed or curved for special effects in achieving a certain design style of course. Certain design styles may be freely combined for a unique effect. Practice, experiment and practice some more. You will eventually find something you like well enough to enter in a show.

There are three basic floral arrangement designs: **Traditional, Modern,** and **Oriental.** All other designs developed from these basics, through the years. Though these styles are most often used for floral arrangements, they can be adapted to show designs for plantings and other floral designs, as well.

Of the three, **Oriental** design is historically the oldest of all flower arranging. This is the earliest recorded form of flower design. Being so old, it is naturally very symbolic and has many traditions behind each design component. As with many Oriental arts, a restrained simplicity is the main keynote. An **Oriental** design can have as few as three items in the entire arrangement, or as many as a dozen flowers, foliage, branches, etc. When only three elements are used, the tallest is "heaven," the middle size is "man," and the lower

branch is "Earth." These elements may be expressed in many different kinds of plants, flowers or foliage. When other elements are added, they descend in secondary lines: "mountain," "meadow," and finally "helpers" that fill in. Learning to create a design that is almost stark in its simplicity takes awhile, but is well worth the effort. Mastery of **Oriental** design means that all other designs will seem very easy.

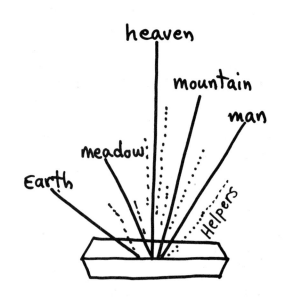

Traditional design goes back centuries to the days when a bouquet of flowers was just shoved into a container with the arranger just hoping for the best. Gradually, a sense of design emerged, but gardeners still used masses of color or a massive amount of flowers and foliage to achieve the effect. **Flemish** bouquets, often depicted in late Renaissance paintings, show the studied casualness of good traditional design in massing lots of color and a variety of flowers to create a pleasing arrangement. **Victorian** design became more florid and flossy, with the addition of lace, ribbons and other accessories. Though the design was slightly more symmetrical by then, so you can see the design to a formal **Victorian** bouquet or nosegay. By **Colonial** times, the traditional design had become more restrained, though the massing of flowers and colors remained as ornate as ever. This design style is the great-grandparent of today's **Oval** arrangement.

Modern design is often characterized as stark and sharp-edged, utilizing unusual color schemes, or black-and-white, or white-on-white. But **Modern** design can also be humorous, brightly

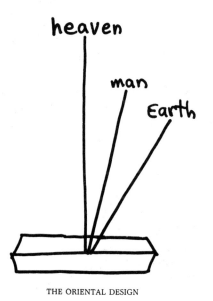

THE ORIENTAL DESIGN

colored, and very attractive. Though a difficult design form to carry off with living plants, it can be quite successful with practice. **Modern** design styles are suitable to unusual plants that would not be comfortable in a more traditional setting. Almost all design forms listed below can be "modernized" to fit this style.

The sub-genus of floral design include the **Oval Design**, descendent of the **Traditional**. Massive foliage may still be in use here, with lavish use of color and variety of foliage, to create the **Oval** look. A formal container could be successfully used with an oval design. Keep the outer edges of the **Oval** light, so it does not overpower the focal point of the design. While this design *seems* to be one of just massing flowers, it is important to keep a good design in mind, and not to overcrowd the flowers used.

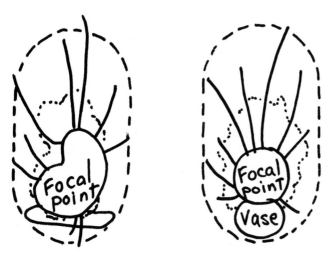

THE OVAL DESIGN

The **Horizontal** design follows the base line of the arrangement to stay low to the base, rather than rising too high above it. This design can be very pretty for dining tables and other areas where the floral arrangement should not get in the way of people. With space limitations in a floral show,

a good **Horizontal** design is often difficult to achieve, but it can be done. Experiment at home with this style.

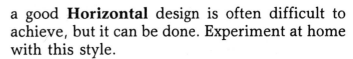

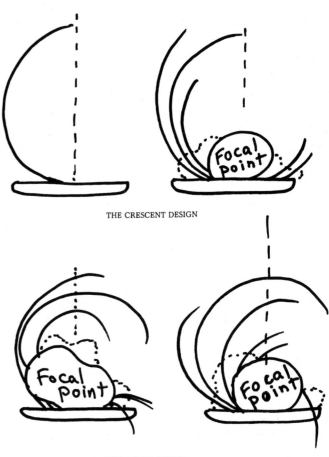

THE CRESCENT DESIGN

THE CIRCLE DESIGN

The **Crescent** and the **Circle Designs** are "kissing cousins" where the difference may depend on your design elements. Usually, the **Crescent** is a more open arrangement, in a crescent moon shape, with a small "S" to keep the design open. The **Circle** may take the eye in a full bull's eye circle, either with curved foliage, or with a circular background. The **Crescent** may flow to the right or the left, as desired. The **Circle** can be designed much like a **Crescent** (that is, as a crescent moon shape, filled in with foliage) or in an old-fashioned design in which the lines radiate from the center of the arrangement.

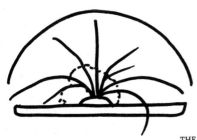

THE HORIZONTAL DESIGN

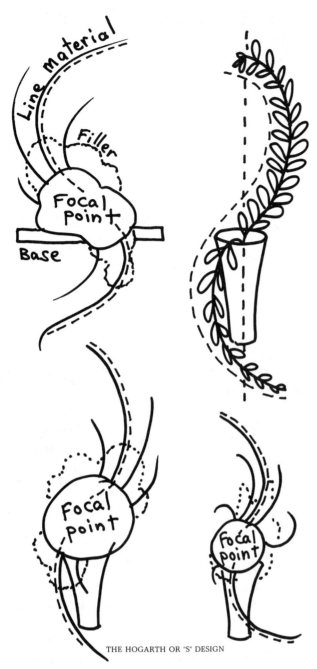

Triangle arrangements are the most common and easiest of all designs to make. They may be made any size, and are very pleasing to the eye. Usually, with a **Triangle** design, all stems radiate from the same place to create a unity. A **Triangle** may have foliage sticking beyond the "triangle" design itself, but not too far.

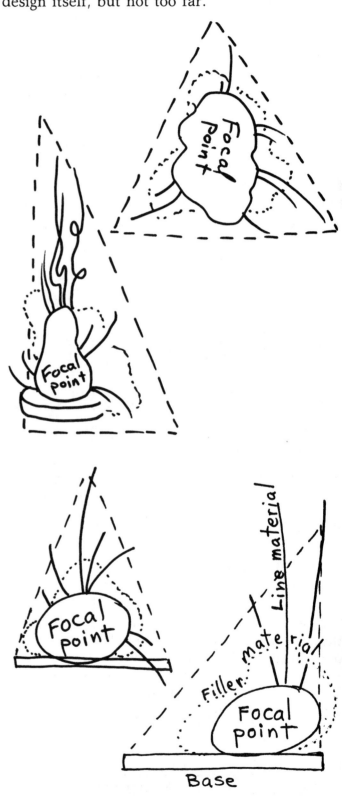

THE HOGARTH OR "S" DESIGN

William Hogarth, English artist of the 1600's, is popularly supposed to have designed the **"S" Curve** or **Hogarth** design style. Also known as the **"Line of Beauty"** it needs a tall container or arrangement to show it off well. This design should not be done in short containers, but it can be successfully done on a base large enough to display the "S" properly in a nearly flat design.

All these designs require practice to achieve them in floral arrangements; using these design styles with living plants often requires imagination and a great deal of interpretation. Also, many times a successful creative design will incorporate elements from several design styles. Don't be afraid to try!

THE TRIANGLE DESIGN

The Artists' List of Color Schemes

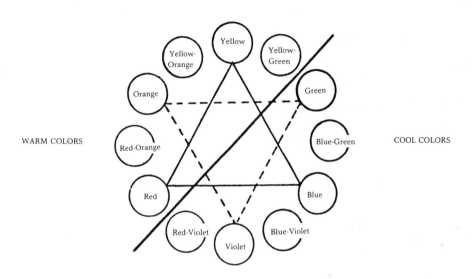

WARM COLORS

COOL COLORS

1. WHITE & OFF WHITE: A colorless scheme must be something special, and used carefully with plants; otherwise the design can look "dead" unless used with discretion.

2. BLACK & WHITE: A sophisticated combination, but these extremes in light and dark are not easy to work with in plant designs unless ingeniously handled.

3. NEUTRAL or EARTHY: Warm or cool grays, beige, ochre, sienna, umber, olive drab, light grayed blues, all earth tones are good colors for backgrounds, or used as "neutralizers" to weld bright, powerful colors together. In the right context, gold and silver are neutrals.

4. MONOCHROME: The use of only one color, in a single or variety of shades and tints, can be very beautiful if handled well.

5. ANALOGOUS: The most popular of all color schemes, the use of tints and shades of adjacent color-wheel neighbors is fun to work with in plants. Care should be taken to use, for instance, all the red-purples and pink-purples in a design, without adding blue-purple.

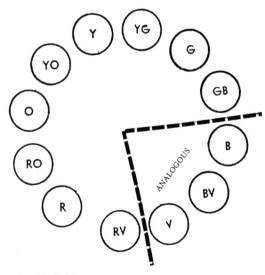

ANALOGOUS COLOR SCHEME: Red-violet, Red, Red-orange or Blue-green, Blue,

Blue-violet or Red-orange, Orange, Yellow-orange, Yellow, etc.

85

6. COMPLIMENTARY: Opposing colors on the color wheel make harmony from contrast. For example, red and green are complimentary, and may be used effectively in tones and shades, such as a deep red with light spring green, or a pink with dark green.

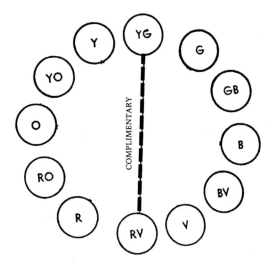

COMPLIMENTARY COLOR SCHEME: Red-violet & Yellow-green or Green-blue &

Red-orange or Yellow-orange & Blue-violet, etc.

7. SPLIT COMPLIMENTARY: Use of three colors, two on one side of the color wheel (say, a blue-green and a blue-violet) and one color from the opposite side of the wheel (say, an orange).Used with correct shading, this can be a stunning color scheme.

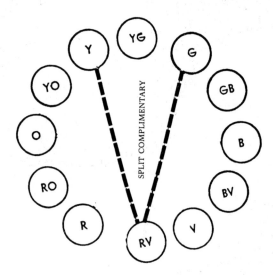

SPLIT COMPLIMENTARY COLOR SCHEME: Green & Yellow-green with Red or Red-violet;

Yellow & Yellow-orange with Violet or Blue-violet, etc.

8. PRIMARY or TRIAD: The basic primary colors (red, blue, yellow) or any triad (three colors in an exact triangle from each other) on the color wheel may seem very primitive, but look around and see how many color schemes are actually primary or triad colors in varying shades. Example: light pink and yellow print blouse with a Navy blue suit.

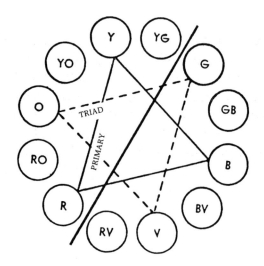

TRIAD COLOR SCHEME: Yellow-orange, Green-blue, & Red-violet or Red-orange,

Yellow-green & Blue-violet, etc.

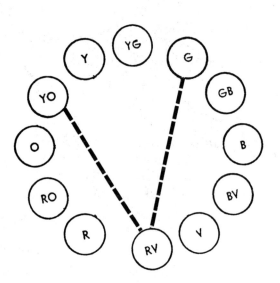

WIDE SPLIT COMPLIMENTARY: Green & Yellow with Red, Red-violet or Violet;

Yellow-orange & Red-orange with Blue-violet, Blue or Green-blue

9. MULTICHROME or POLYCHROME: A mixture of many colors, found in Persian carpets, English gardens, tartan plaids, Imari prints, etc. Having many colors to work with is an attractive freedom, but one which should not be abused. Each color should add to the overall effect in some way, however small. The handling of many colors should be very carefully planned.

10. EXPLORATORY COLOR SCHEMES: This is an area of color which invites experiment with pattern, texture and color not usually found in normal or mundane designs. While such color schemes are unconventional and have unfamiliar values, the design should not use strange color schemes for shock value alone. Nothing is gained by such tactics. Always try this color scheme out on friends before entering it in a show!

—*Bjo Trimble*

Sinningia Canescens

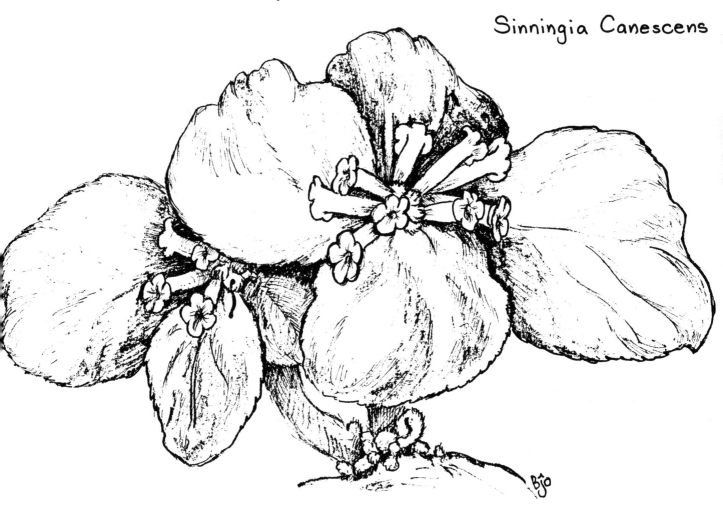

Columnea "Sonnenafgang"

Bjo

*"C'mon, a judge is supposed to **study** an exhibit, but this is ridiculous!"*

CHAPTER X

Judging the Design Division

This, I feel, is the most important chapter in this book. Because there has been so much controversy in judging show designs, and many, many times judges themselves feel a little inadequate when asked to judge the Design Division.

My advice to any judge who does not feel qualified, is: whenever you get an invitation to judge designs, be honest. Drop the show chairman a note, requesting that you not be placed on the panel for judging designs.

Designs are not just tossed together in a few

minutes. You can groom a dozen show plants in less time than you can create a design. So let's give these designers a fair chance: don't judge their designs unless you really feel qualified to do so. I know that all judges are honest enough to admit this. However, in close to thirty years of judging African violet and other gesneriad shows as well as other flower shows, I have many times judged on a panel where both of the other judges readily admitted they knew absolutely nothing about design. I'm not talking about 10 or 20 or 25 years ago; I'm talking about last year, 1984, where judges have admitted they didn't know anything about the Design Division. This is not fair to the designer. I can't emphasize too much: PLEASE BE FAIR! If you want to judge a Design Division, study it, read books, learn your different elements, principles of design, learn what to look for in a design, go to shows, take extra judges' courses.

In all judges' courses, there is a section for design. If you cannot answer the test questions readily, go look them up. We have three judges' manuals: *The Handbook for Judges and Exhibitors* written by Ruth Carey for the AVSA; *The Handbook for Judges* by Frances Batchellor for AGGS; and the *Saintpaulia International Judges Guide*. These books are valuable to all judges and exhibitors—put them to good use.

"Looks like somebody doesn't agree with our judgment!"

This article was published in the November issue of the *PGS News*, 1984. It was written by Alan La Vergne, editor of that newsletter. I have used the wording with a change from "plants" to "design," but the whole concept is so good I would like to share it with my readers.

On Being Judged

AGGS and other plant societies give classes on judging, but nobody gives classes on being judged. It's not always a comfortable experience, and if we are to get full value from it, we must go with the right attitude.
Here are some things to keep in mind:

1. Beauty is in the eye of the beholder. It's trite but true. Try to find someone who agrees with you about everything. Just try. After that, you won't think it surprising any longer that you sometimes disagree with the judging.

2. Judges have to *judge*. No matter how close the call, no matter how equal the design, they have to make a decision. Are they being paid for it? Does judging make them popular? Have a little sympathy for the judges, who are doing the best they can.

3. The design is being judged, not you. If your design doesn't get a blue ribbon, it doesn't mean that you are morally inferior, or dumb, or careless. The judges just liked another design better, or perhaps the winner interpreted the class, and projected the picture more clearly. They weren't passing judgment on your taste, background, intelligence, ethics or paternity.

4. Being a good sport pays dividends later. After all, when YOU win best in show, you don't want other people grousing about the judging and detracting from YOUR pleasure in winning. Set a good example NOW.

5. Learn from it. In the disappointment of the moment, it will be hard to benefit from criticism, no matter how constructive, but later on, when the show is history, those comments can be very helpful toward getting awards in the future..

6. It's a show; the whole idea is to show off beautiful designs and plants, to share your enjoyment of them. Let your enjoyment show. People look at all the entries, not just the winners. Everything gets appreciated and admired, regardless of the awards.

7. Finally, and most important, the design itself is the reward, not the ribbon. If you have done your best, and you like the end results, be assured the members and public will enjoy your efforts.
If you have that, who needs a ribbon?

Printed with the kind permission of Mr. Alan La Vergne, Editor of *The Peninsula Gesneriad News*, San Francisco, California.

When a judge accepts a judging assignment for a club, the Judges' chairman will send out the schedule well in advance of the show date. This gives the judge time to study the rules of that particular organization, and clarify all classes and headings for the design division. This is the division this chapter will deal with exclusively. If a judge is to judge a class depicting a 'Foreign Film', it is their duty to read and be knowledgeable about several different types of films. In my own experience I haven't seen a movie of any kind for more than ten years, so it would certainly behoove me to do some research. My daughter is an avid movie 'buff' so I had ample information to draw from, as well as film clips. This is just an example of how easy it is to learn about any class to be judged. Look to your friends, relatives, members and of course the public libraries are a great source of information.

Offer to be a clerk for a show, if you are not asked to be a judge. Go to local shows; visit other shows. Naturally a clerk can't be close enough to hear what the judges say, but when you are looking at a design, take the time to look and figure out what the designer was trying to tell you.

If you are entering a show, the first thing you do is study the show schedule. Don't just look at it; don't just read it; STUDY IT! Particularly the Design Division, if that is what you are going to enter. That is what we are talking about here. Your design MUST fit the rules, and not just suit yourself. You have to interpret the show schedule as best you can.

If you have trouble, consult the show chairman or the schedule chairman. Don't wait until the day of the show, when you have placed your entry, to inquire. Do it well ahead of time, so you can plan your design to fit the rules of that particular show.

All shows do not have the same rules. The gesneriad shows have all their rules set down by the American Gloxinia and Gesneriad Society; the African violet shows follow rules set down by the Ruth Carey judges' handbook mentioned before; Saintpaulia International have their own rules. Basicallly, they have similar rules, but whichever club is sponsoring the show currently being judged is the important one. It is the duty of all judges to read and know the specific rules governing that show.

Gesneriad shows usually have a class or division for African violets and AVSA shows have a division for the 'other' gesneriads. This is why a knowledge of these handbooks is important to exhibitors as well as judges.

The flower show SCHEDULE is the LAW of the show. This fact holds true in all types of flower shows. Judges MUST study the schedule of every show they judge. Each club or organization has a different schedule, so judges are required to study and know the rules governing each and every show to be judged.

Interpretation of the schedule is just as important to a judge as it is to an exhibitor. There must be an accord between the two.

All judges try to be fair in judging. Most of them have at one time or another entered designs in a show or shows. I am sure they would like to give each entry a blue ribbon. That being impossible, they do the next best thing, they do their utmost to be fair to each and every entry, in selecting the best design in each class. Judges are, however, only human. They have been trained in their field, and are willing to place themselves open for public criticism by agreeing to be part of the judging panel.

Here are some guidelines set down by one very qualified source:

Suggestions on Judging Arrangements

In judging floral show arrangements judges must first and foremost remember that arrangements to be judged should not be touched or handled in any manner. One false move in turning a base or accessory can end in disaster. Judges should ask themselves, "Did the exhibitor interpret the class in the show schedule correctly?" I find often this is the biggest abuse. The schedule is not read as was intended and one must always remember the schedule is the law of the show. So an exhibitor should take time to read carefully and if it is unclear, inquire exactly what is meant by the individual who wrote the schedule.

I once had the experience of judging arrangements at a show where the class called for a "Bit of China." Most individuals who entered the class brought out their finest

"Well, according to the schedule,
    it definitely qualifies for 'Bit of China' "

Dresden china. The china exhibit was breathtaking—however, only one or two exhibitors got the correct meaning from the schedule and had beautiful arrangements with rickshaws and delicate Chinese figures to compliment their theme. Perhaps the class schedule would have been better understood if the word "country" or "old world" were included in the class title.

Judges who undertake the task of judging should observe courteously, weigh carefully, consider soberly and decide impartially any and every design concept or arrangement individually.

Judges must take time to study a design or arrangement. Never take for granted that first glance can determine a winner. Some important questions which may arise in the judge's mind are as follows: "Does the design or arrangement show aesthetic beauty in color, design, scale, form, balance and harmony?"

A judge must work in harmony with all members on the panel, discussion should be free and open, but one member should never be allowed to dominate in making a final decision. Observe details of arrangements, and consider also if the exhibitor has followed the specific rules in class entered as to size, background or any other rule stated in the schedule.

Are the delicate violet blossoms fresh and appropriately used to suggest harmony and accent where it is intended?

Are accessories properly used so they become a part of the design but do not overpower it? Are they in proper proportion?

Bases and backgrounds can lend great beauty to arrangements or they can create great problems. Both are important and should be in harmony with the arrangement. They should never stand out as objects, but fit in as complimentary accessories in the design one wishes to achieve.

Your creative ability with thought, study and practice can bring you the great personal satisfaction of a blue ribbon arrangement.

—Anne Tinari
Lifetime Judge
Designer and Teacher
President, AVSA
Co-owner, Tinari Greenhouses

So that you may better understand what kind of people make these judgments, here are the qualifications, drastically edited for easier understanding, of Ruth G. Carey's list in *The African Violent Handbook for Judges and Exhibitors*:

Qualifications of a flower show judge:

1. Knowledge: Judges should have a thorough knowledge of the many varieties of the plant or flower they are judging; should know in what respects they are similar or different. Some judges are better than others, with the same training. JUDGMENT reflects personal experience, knowledge and training. It is not possible to have a specific rule that will apply to every problem or situation a judge may encounter. Judges are not perfect and neither can there be an exact arithmetical formula for judging.

2. Experience: This is the most important qualification, and should include actually growing old and new varieties of the flowers and plants being judged. It is also helpful to have knowledge and experience in judging the species, as some are judged as symmetrical growing plants, and some are grown and judged as trailing varieties. An important qualification for judges is that they should be active members of the organization which is sponsoring the show, or have a judge's certificate in that area.

3. Fairness: Judges should be unprejudiced in all decisions, and should be led only by the rules and regulations laid down by the show schedule, and see that each entry meets the requirements. Judges should accept a judging assignment *only* when they feel totally qualified to do so. Judges who have never done an arrangement or design should *not* try to judge this category; it is not fair or even courteous to the hard-working exhibitor.

4. Courage: All judges need courage; it is not easy to place your reputation and decisions in the public eye. Sometimes it is easier to give awards

than to meet the opposition of other judges. It takes courage to stick to your decision if you feel it is correct. Judges should not strain at technicalities, but should be willing to explain their decisions.

5. Tact: A judge should be tolerant of new judges, and novices in the show. One judge should not dominate the others, but remember, judging is teamwork.

6. Kindness: Remarks should build up, not tear down the exhibitor. Judges should criticize only to improve. Kindness is like the family cat; if you try to give it away, very likely it will come back.

Printed from The AVSA Handbook for Judges & Exhibitions
with the kind permission of the author, Ruth G. Carey.

Judges should try to 'see' what the designer had in mind; to understand why the exhibit was set up in the manner displayed. The title of the design is the first clue to the mood or theme of the class. As Ruth Carey put it so well, "Judges should be unbiased in every decision. Look for beauty."

Remember, the decision of the judges is final; not even the judges themselves are allowed to change an award, once the decision has been made by the panel.

There have been instances where the judges chairman has asked the panel of judges to do a critique of the design division. The exhibitors must be present and consent to the discussion. This is extremely beneficial to new clubs and affiliates

"Would you believe it's part of the design?"

"Maybe Betty is too soft-hearted to be a judge!"

producing their first show. The judges must show tact, consideration for the exhibitors' experience, and kindness to encourage them to continue entering designs.

Designs are judged differently in every show — this follows as true because the designs are different, and different people are on each panel. Each schedule chairman may add their own club rules as long as they do not conflict with rules of the organization they are affiliated with. The freedom to selects different themes and titles permits a club to add distinction and variety to each show. This is why it is so important for judges to study the schedule thoroughly before the day of the actual judging. Design receives the most points in judging all entries in the design division. The following is my procedure for viewing concepts in design:

1. Artistic or creative design of plants or flowers in the arrangement.

2. Compatibility of all materials used in the design.

3. Condition — are all flowers and plants clean and fresh.

4. Do colors blend or contrast to produce balance and achieve unity.

5. Distinction and originality; perhaps it is the spark of imagination in the mind of the exhibitor which makes the difference. Distinction and originality go hand-in-hand. It is not possible to have distinction without originality.

Distinction is concerned with superiority.

Distinctiveness is concerned with separation or difference.

The factors to consider in judging design are

usually, line, form, balance, contrast, scale, dominance, texture, rhythm and pattern. All these factors are interlocked with the other judging points. For instance, does the use of color promote balance in the design, or is it just a spot of color at one side of the arrangement?

Proportion and scale mean the completed design will have a good relationship between the plants or flowers, the container and any figurines used with the base and background.

Balance is the stability of the design, so that it looks secure enough to not fall apart at a touch. Balance or weight of a design may be symmetrical or assymetrical; an equal balance of form and size in every direction of the design; or an unequal balance achieved by use of line material and accessories.

Accessories, point of interest, impact, figurines, and many other ways to follow the theme, catch the eye and create interest. This is an area to be thoroughly and critically explored. Proportion is of utmost importance when using anything other than plants or blossoms in a design. Any item must not detract from the beauty but serve to enhance the overall design. The color should blend with the theme being used in a subtle but interesting way to highlight the arrangement. It is my considered opinion that more than one figurine in a design is too much. I have seen it done successfully, but only on rare occasions. So much for my opinion.

Several years ago I entered several designs in the Ventura County African Violet Society Show. Their show committee included a chairman called the Show Coordinator. Their duty was to check all entries after they were placed the evening before the judging. All horticultural entries were checked for the correct classes and the design division was checked to see that all entries followed the rules and theme. I had a call from the chairman to tell me that one of my designs would be disqualified as it was placed. I had time

the next morning to change the design before judging was to begin. I was happy to take home a blue ribbon, and was grateful to the person who called me. I would recommend all show chairmen to appoint such a coordinator for all shows.

Putting on a show is such a busy time and everyone is busy and excited, to say the least, so having a person to check all exhibits is certainly a very worthwhile venture.

I've shared my knowledge and experience in floral design – the rest is up to you. Remember the advice of the *Saintpaulia International Judge's Guide*: "One of the most potent weapons for learning is the well regulated, carefully conducted experiment. And so, through experiment, and study, and experience, come knowledge. It does take time."

It takes courage to try, and even more courage to fail. Out of many failures will eventually come success. I could write a bigger book on the failures I have had, but it has been worth the effort. Along the way, I have met some beautiful people, seen well-staged shows, grown and worked with exquisite plants, and enjoyed every minute of the experience.

Glossary/Index

a:

ACCESSORIES: **IX**
AGGS: American Gloxinia & Gesneriad Society
AIR DRYING: **VII**
AMERICAN CAN COMPANY: **IV**
AMERICAN GLOXINIA & GESNERIAD SOCIETY: **X**
ANALOGOUS: Used to describe colors which are neighboring or next to one another on an artist's color wheel. **IX**
ANGEL FEATHERS: Skeletonized leaves.
ANIMALS, LIVE: Do not use in a design for a show! **II**
ANTIQUES:Do not use in a design for a show! **II**
AQUARIUM GRAVEL: This is safe to use because it has already been thoroughly sterilized for live fish **VI**
AQUATIC SNAILS: **III**
ARTISTIC PLANTINGS: **V, VI**
ASHLEY, DORIS: *xi*
AVSA: African Violet Society of America
AVSA JUDGES & EXHIBITORS HANDBOOK: **IX**

the design. **III, V**
BATCHELLOR, FRANCES: *xi*, **X**
BEASLEY, HENRY: **VII**
BELLY-BUTTON CORSAGE: **IV**
BIG-TOE CORSAGE: **IV**
BIRDS, LIVE: Do not use in a design for a show! **II**
BLEED: Some plants, when their stems are cut, will "bleed," causing stains or stickiness which must be cleaned up immediately. Bleeding of stems into water used for an arrangement can cloud the water and contaminate it for other plants. **II, III**
BODY FLOWERS: **I, IV**
"BONFIRE" NEMATANTHUS
BOTTLE GARDEN: **I, IV, VI**
BOUTONNIERE: Literally, "buttonhole" or a flower worn in the buttonhole.
BUBBLE BOWL: **I, III, IV**
BUBBLE GARDEN: Same as BUBBLE BOWL: **I, III, IV**
BUD VASE: Small container designed to hold one flower, or only a few flowers.
BURLAP: Useful as a neutral, textured background or to cover a base or to hold root balls.

B:

"BABY" EUCALYPTUS: The smaller branches, with dainty leaves. **V, VII**
BACKGROUND: The draping, box, or other form placed in back of a design to help set it off. **III, IV, V**
BACKGROUND MATERIAL: This can be either the fabric used to drape on a background, or the foliage and line material used as a background for

C:

CABINET SPECIMEN: Rock collectors take very good care of their special gem and mineral specimens, usually displaying them in a cabinet. **VIII**

CALYX: The whorl of leaves forming the husk or outer casing of a bud. **IV**

CAREY, RUTH G.: **X**

CASKET PIECE: The covering of flowers placed on top of a funeral casket.

CHARACTER: The aggregate of distinctive features of any thing's essential peculiarity; quality delineating, describing, symbolizing. **IX**

"CHICKEN LEG": When a wired stem is taped badly, it presents a lumpy or "chicken leg" appearance. This is to be avoided. **IV**

CIRCLE: In design, this is an arrangement which curves, or in some other manner, achieves almost

a full circle.

CLASS: In flower shows, a CLASS is usually the same thing as a DIVISION or a CATEGORY. **VI**

CLUSTERING: A method of achieving a lot of color or foliage where needed, by bunching or clustering a group of small plants to look like a larger one. **VI**

COLONIAL: A type of floral design seen in arrangements or in nosegays: a seemingly informal collection of many flowers in an artless design. Also: VICTORIAN, TRADITIONAL, FLEMISH **IV**

COLOR, USE OF: **IX**

COMPLIMENTARY: Colors opposite one another on an artist's color wheel. **IX**

CONDITION: **IV, VI**

CONTAINER: The choice of a container is often as important to a good design as the choice of flower and foliage.

CONTRAST: To bring out strongly differences in form, color, etc., and thus produce a striking effect. **IX**

CORSAGE: A gathering or bouquet of flowers especially designed to be worn on the body. **IV**

CORSAGE ASSEMBLY: **IV**

CORSAGE BAG: A cellophane bag, with foil insert, made especially to carry corsages. Florists often add a bit of shredded cellophane or waxed paper to protect the flowers even more.

CORSAGE BOX: A box, usually foil-covered, made especially to carry corsages. Usually some shredded cellophane or waxed paper is added to protect flowers.

CORSAGE-MAKING: **IV**

CORSAGE PIN: A sharp 3" long pin, with a pearlized or colored pear-shaped head, used to hold corsages onto clothing. **IV**

COVER, TERRARIUM: Sometimes a show schedule demands a cover on a terrarium—be sure to check before the show. **VI**

CRANE, ESTELLE: **X**

CRESCENT: A design often interchangeable with the "CIRCLE", in which curved line material or other components of the design may suggest a crescent.

CRYSTAL SPECIMEN: Usually a rockhound's pride and joy is a really fine group or single crystal specimen, which also makes a beautiful addition to a show design, if you can get it. **VIII**

CROSS: Horticultural term for "cross-breeding" plants. **VI**

CYPRESS KNEE: Part of the root growth of cypress trees growing in water. See cover of this book for an example of a cypress knee used in a design. *iv*, **VIII**

D:

DISH GARDEN: Any miniature garden which is planted in a shallow container, such as a large dish, a tray, etc. A dish garden may also be a "HANGING GARDEN" if it is suspended in a hangar. **VI**

DESIGN DIVISION: The section of a flower or plant show in which the exhibitor utilizes creative design with designated plants or flowers, often for a specific theme. Term is interchangeable in this book with "section" and "category."

DESIGNER: One who designs; not necessarily synonymous with one who exhibits.

DIXIE AFRICAN VIOLET SOCIETY: III

DIXIE NEWS: III

DORMANT: Some plants can go dormant, or totally inactive, for lengths of time, and revive later to become beautiful and alive.

DRAPING: The background of a design is often covered with a draping of fabric, which should add to, not detract from the design. **III, V**

DRIED MATERIAL: Any plant material which will hold its shape if not always its color when dried. **III**

DRIFTWOOD: The designer's favorite! Any interesting piece of wood found on a beach or river bank. **II, III, VI, VII, VIII**

DRUGGIST'S GENERAL RECEIPT BOOK: VII

E:

EGGS, REAL: Use jellybeans in a design, instead. **II**

EXHIBIT: A design or plant placed on exhibit in a floral show.

EXHIBITOR: One who enters an exhibit (plant, flower, floral design, etc.) in a show.

F:

FERMATE: A type of agricultural "soot" used in design like Fuller's earth, which see. *II, III*

FIBROUS ROOTED: Thread-like filament structure.

FIGURINES: The proportion of a figurine is very important to a design; as in wearing jewelry, discretion should be applied to the placement of figurines in a design. **VI**

FILLER, FILLER MATERIAL: Anything used to "fill in" a design in any way. Foliage, driftwood, even draping can sometimes be filler material. **VII**

FIRESIDE LIBRARY OF USEFUL KNOWLEDGE: VII

FISH, LIVE: Do not use in an underwater design. **II**

FLAT LEAVES, WIRING: II

"FLAT" POUF: IV

FLEMISH: A design form using massed or massive amounts of flowers, with no set pattern, but lots of color. Also: TRADITIONAL, COLONIAL, VICTORIAN

FLESHMAN, KEN & FRANCES: *xi*

"FLORAL DESIGN POINTERS": IV

FLORAL GLUE: A spray-on glue that is effective for short-term use in designs. Heed warning on aerosol can about breathing the spray! **IV**

FLORAL FOAM: A type of porous material which can be cut and shaped to fit inside containers to act as a sponge and hold water for cut flowers. Also useful to a limited degree as a substitute pin frog. Found under several brand names in floral supply houses, some hobby shops. **II**

FLORISTS' REVIEW, THE: IV

FLORIST'S WIRE: This comes in several thicknesses, the most popular being #20, 22, 28. If you can obtain only one wire size, #28 is generally used. Florist's wire comes bare and covered with a colored thread. **I, IV**

FLOWERS, WIRING: **IV**

"FLUFFY" POUF: **IV**

FOCAL POINT: The main point in any design is the FOCAL POINT, without which the design may be merely a floral arrangement for everyday use.

FOLIAGE, WIRING: **IV**

FULLER'S EARTH: A type of dark, loamy earth used in potting mixes, and by designers for darkening or dulling arrangement bases, backgrounds, and containers. (HEED WARNING IN CHAPTER II) **II, III**

G:

GARDENS: See DISH GARDENS, HANGING GARDENS, BOTTLE GARDENS, RAIN GARDENS

GEL, SILICA: **VII**

GESNERIAD SAINTPAULIA INTERNATIONAL: An organization

"GEMMY": In rockhound slang, any gemstone which can be cut and polished. **VIII**

GLOXINIA & GESNERIAD SOCIETY, AMERICAN: **VIII**

GSI: Gesneriad Saintpaulia International

GLYCERINE: **VII**

h:

HAIR PIECE: Any flowers arranged so as to be worn in the hair. **IV**

HANDBOOK: Usually meaning a specific handbook written for flower show judges and exhibitors. See: THE HANDBOOK FOR JUDGES & EXHIBITORS, THE HANDBOOK FOR JUDGES.

HANDY HINTS FOR CORSAGE-MAKING: **IV**

HANGING GARDEN: Any of the miniature gardens in dishes or containers that can be hung on a holder or from the ceiling by means of a macrame hanger or by monofilament lines.

HARDEN, HARDEN OFF: **IX**

HOGARTH: A classic "S" curved design supposed to have been devised by the artist William Hogarth (1697-1764) as the perfect roccoco aesthetic arrangement.

HORIZONTAL: A design which follows the horizontal line material, instead of reaching for height.

HORTICULTURE DIVISION: Along with the Design Division, floral shows have other categories in which one may enter plants; this is one of them **VI**

HYGROSCOPIC: Tending to absorb water out of the atmosphere.

J:

JELLYBEANS: Use in a design instead of real bird's eggs. **II**

JORGENSEN, LINDA: *xi*

JUDGE: In this book a person qualified to judge flowers or plants; not always synonymous with a judge who knows about floral design.

JUDGES, HANDBOOK FOR: **X**

m:

MATERIAL: Always used in this book to mean the plants, foliage or blossoms being used in a design.

McCOY, JOHN: *v, xi*

MECHANICS: The actual structure or mechanism, hidden by the design, which holds the creation together. **III**

MINI-NOSEGAY: A small bouquet to be carried or even worn as a corsage on the index finger. **I, IV**

MODERN: In design, this can be a free-form arrangement of elements, rather than the more rigid disciplines of other design styles; it can also mean squared, stark lines and experimental color schemes.

MONOCHROME: Used to describe the use of only one color.

MORRIS, CHARLES: **VII**

"MOUSE EAR": A small loop of ribbon, wired and taped, to add to a corsage or other design for a spot of color. **IV**

MULTICHROME: A mixture of many colors. Also: POLYCHROME

k:

KAHRMANN, DOROTHY: *xi*

KEEPSAKES: Do not use in a design for show! **II**

KINETICS: **III**

KING, JOSEPH: **IV**

KISTLER, WILLIAM: **IV**

KNIFE: The preferred tool to use in most design work, instead of scissors. A florist's knife is designed for such work; a paring knife or pocketknife will do as well. **II, VII**

l:

LANGE, LOREE: *xi*

LARGE LEAF & CALYX WIRING: **IV**

LA VERGNE, ALAN: *xi*, **X**

LIFETIME JUDGE: An honor bestowed upon AVSA judges who have reached a certain level of expertise.

LILLIQUIST, MADGE: *xi*

LINE MATERIAL: The foliage, driftwood or other material used to create the primary line, establishing the height of the design or arrangement. **III, V, VII**

LIVE ANIMALS: Do not use in a design! **II**

n:

NAMED VARIETIES: When a plant breeds true, it may be named and registered. **VI**

NET: An extra fine net is used to make professional florist's "poufs" but ordinary nylon net will do if nothing else is available. Net poufs help prevent the face from brushing corsage flowers. Net may also be used to drape over backgrounds to soften color or line, when necessary. **II, IV**

NEUTRAL: A color which does not impinge on the design; usually a dull or drab color, or an earth tone.

NOSEGAY: A round bouquet of flowers, usually an assortment with some of the components chosen for their pleasing scent. In earlier times, the nosegay or "tussy mussy" would contain herbs, such as rosemay or mint, popularly supposed to hold off illness, as well as the odors of the day. Now a favorite bouquet design for garden parties, debutantes and weddings. **IV**

NYLON HOSE: Used to hold a root ball in place for a temporary planting. **I**

O:

ORIENTAL: Historically the earliest and most enduring study of floral design and arrangement. Each flower, piece of foliage, etc., has a special and specific meaning, with simplicity being the main point of the design.

OVAL: A design descendant from Victorian arrangements, usually requiring lavish use of foliage to fill in the shape.

P:

PARENT PLANT: The plant off which cuttings were taken to produce identical plants. **III**

PENINSULA GESNERIAD SOCIETY NEWS: **X**

PERMANENT ARTISTIC PLANTINGS: **VI**

PGS NEWS: **X**

PHANTOM LEAVES:

PLANTLET: A small plant, usually accepted as a plant grown from a gesneriad cutting, instead of a seed. See also: SEEDLING

PLIERS: Use pliers when twisting florist's wire, instead of using fingers. **II**

POLYCHROME: A mixture of many colors. Also: MULTICHROME

POTTING MIX: African violet potting mix is available at nurseries, and is advised for use in miniature plantings.

POTTING SOIL: See POTTING MIX

"POUF": **IV, VII**

PRESERVING: Drying flowers and foliage, or in some other manner preserving them for later use in a design. **VII**

PRESSING FLOWERS: **VII**

PRIMARY: **The three basic colors: red, yellow, blue on an artist's color wheel.**

PROPORTION: **IX, VIII**

R:

RAFFLE: A favorite fund-raiser for clubs and conventions. **VI**

RAIN GARDEN: Another name for BOTTLE GARDEN **VI**

RAIN WATER: If unpolluted, this is the finest water to use. **VII**

REGISTERED: If a plant breeds true, it may be registered and named. **VI**

REGULATIONS, SHOW: See SHOW SCHEDULE

RHYTHM: The correlation and interdependence of parts, producing a harmonious whole; movement marked by regulated succession of accented and unaccented elements; a measured flow. **IX**

RHIZOME: Prostate rootstock.

ROCK CUTTING: The first step in the process of cutting, grinding and polishing a semi-precious gemstone. **VIII**

ROCKHOUND: A person whose hobby is picking up rocks, polishing them, and giving them away; as opposed to a plant fancier, whose hobby is obtaining plants, starting cuttings, and giving them away. **VIII**

ROOT BALL: The ball or collection of plant roots; most gesneriads can be removed from their pots for a limited time without harm, if the root ball is protected as described in Chapter I.

ROOT KNOT: A twisted knot of dried plant or tree,

usually from the roots, that can be used in a floral design. **II**

"ROUND" POUF: **IV**

RULES, SHOW: See SHOW SCHEDULE

S:

SAINTPAULIA INTERNATIONAL: **X**

SAINTPAULIA INTERNATIONAL JUDGES HANDBOOK: **X**

SALES TABLE: A favorite fund-raiser for clubs and conventions. **VI**

SCALE: A condition of equilibrium in both math and floral design, where the value of a figure (or a design component) varies in geometric progression according to its serial place. **IX**

"S" CURVE: See HOGARTH

SECTION: Used interchangeably in this book for "division" or "category" of a flower show.

SEEDLING: Gesneriad cuttings will breed true, but seedlings grown from seeds often do not. For that reason, seedlings are not "named" and may not be entered in African violet or gesneriad shows unless they are used in a design, where a named plant is usually not necessary (check show schedule: sometimes a named plant is called for).
V, VI

SEMI-PRECIOUS: Any gemstone which is not one of the more valuable precious stones is considered to be "semi-precious". This category includes garnets, as well as certain non-gem types, such as turquoise. **VIII**

SHOW: In this book, refers only to African violet and other gesneriad shows.

SHOW RULES: See SHOW SCHEDULE

SHOW SCHEDULE: The rules and regulations of a flower show; for this book, only the show schedule of African violet and other gesneriad shows are cited. Show schedules for other floral and plant shows may be quite different, and individual shows may vary drastically, so always ask for any specific show's own schedule of rules.

SILICONIZING: Using silica gel to dry plant life. **VII**

"SMOKY EMERALD" APICIA

SKELETON LEAVES: **VII**

SKELETONIZING: To make skeleton leaves, see **VII**

SLAB: Rockhounds use a diamond-wheel rocksaw to slice large roks into "slabs" so they can be used as is, or cut into smaller pieces to polish as gemstones. Slabs make nice bases for miniature arrangements. **VIII**

SMITH, JESSIE: *xi*, **VI**

SOIL: Any time "soil" is mentioned, it refers to African violet/gesneriad potting mix *only*, not garden dirt.

SOOT: See FULLER'S EARTH, FERMATE

SPACE: The proper place or relationship; the dimensional extent occupied by a body or lying within its limits. **IX**

STABILE: **III**

STABILITY: The power of remaining erect; the freedom from liability to fall over; enduring quality. **IX**

STAMOBILE: **III**

t:

"TAIL": The end of a ribbon, if allowed to show, is a "tail"; most commonly seen in the construction of "mouse ears." **IV**

TALC, TALCUM POWDER: The handiest to use is

baby talcum powder; any kind will do to give a too-shiny container a temporary dull or matte finish. **II, III**

TAPING: The act of wrapping floral tape around a stem or other object. **IV**

TEMPORARY ARTISTIC PLANTINGS: **V**

TERRARIUM: A miniature garden planted in a glass-walled container, such as an aquarium tank, large bubble bowl, etc., that is completely self-contained. A properly planted terrarium needs little or no extra watering, once established. **VI**

TEXTURE: **IX**

THEME: The given subject of a floral show, show category or show division, which may be developed by the designer with variations, within the rules of the show schedule. **III, IX**

TINARI, ANNE & FRANK: *ix, xi,* **X**

TITLE: Some designs need titles or captions to explain their connection with the theme of the show. Usually, a small card, stating the title of the design in readable lettering, will suffice to inform the viewer.

TRADITIONAL: Usually massed or massive design with no set pattern, using many colors and flowers. Also: COLONIAL, VICTORIAN, FLEMISH

"TRAILALONG" AFRICAN VIOLET:

TRAILER: A type of gesneriad with trailing stems and leaves; specifically, an African violet with a trailing growth habit instead of growing in the usual "bouquet" shape.

TREAT, TREATING, TREATED: Used in this book to describe any plant material that has been conditioned, dried, or otherwise changed to use in a design.

TRIAD: Any three colors on an artist's color wheel that are an exact triangle from each other.

TRIANGLE: A design form in triangle shape.

TRIMBLE, JOHN: *v*

TUBER: An underground stem covered with modified buds

TUMBLED ROCK: Rockhounds often "tumble" polish semi-precious stones to create highly polished baroque-shaped gemstones.

TYING FISHING LINE: **III**

U:

UNDERWATER ARRANGEMENT: The same as UNDERWATER DESIGN

UNNAMED: Any seedling or other plant which does not have a name. Many shows will not allow unnamed plants to be entered in any division. **VI**

V:

VARIETY, NAMED: A plant which has bred true long enough to be registered, and named. **VI**

W:

WAGUESPACK, MARGARET: *xi,* **III**

WATERFALL: **VI**

WIRE: See FLORIST'S WIRE. **I, II, IV**

WIRE-CUTTER: A necessary tool when using florist's or chicken wire for designs. **II**

WIRING: The act of adding wire to a stem or flower to strengthen it for a corsage or design. **IV**

WRISTLET: A corsage worn on the wrist. Also, the plastic or elastic band to which the corsage is attached. **I, IV**

Bibliography

African Violet Handbook for Judges and Exhibitors by Ruth G. Carey for African Violet Society of America, Inc.

African Violet Society of America, Inc.
P.O. Box 3609
Beaumont, TX 77704

American Gloxinia and Gesneriad Society Flower Show Manual for Judges and Exhibitors by Frances Batcheller and Estelle Crane

American Gloxinia & Gesneriad Society
P.O. Box 493
Beverly Farms, MA 01915

Saintpaulia International Judges Guide written for Saintpaulia International Society

Gesneriad Society International
and Saintpaulia International
Box 549
Knoxville, TN 37901

Gesneriad Hybridizers' Association
4115 Pillar Drive, Route 1
Whitemore Lake, MI 48189

When inquiring about handbooks or society membership, please remember to include an L.S.A.S.E.* for prompt answer. These organizations are non-profit, and cannot handle heavy postal expense.

*Long (Business-sized) Self-Addressed Stamped Envelope

Giggles strike Jo McCoy & Bjo Trimble during photo session

"What's so funny?"

"I never thought I'd ever write a book!"

"What do you think of being an author, now?"

"It's like having a baby, but the labor is longer!"

Look for these books on

FLORAL DESIGN CONCEPTS

by Ruth Jo McCoy

in the near future:

Camelias
Chrysanthemums
Dahlias
Ferns
Fuschias
Orchids
Roses
Tulips & Other Tuberous Flowers

Tri-Color Press

3963 Wilshire Blvd., Suite 600

Los Angeles, CA 90211

Best
in
Show

◄ • ►

Design
Division

◄ • ►